READING
TEA
LEAVES

READING
TEA
LEAVES

DISCOVER WHAT BREWS IN
YOUR FUTURE

✦ ✦ ✦

APRIL WALL

weldon**owen**

CONTENTS

INTRODUCTION

H UMANS HAVE A deep desire to know what their future
holds. Life can be so chaotic with all its twists and turns.
It's only natural to want a sneak peek into what may be heading
your way. This yearning to see into the future is nothing new.
Going as far back as Mesopotamia, people used divination to
prepare for what was to come, including reading animal entrails
(hieromancy), bones (osteomancy), books (bibliomancy), melted
wax (carromancy), and cheese (tyromancy). Yes, you read that
right—even cheese was once used to divine the mysteries of the
future! Those poor lactose-intolerant practitioners.

But time marches forward, and we developed new tools and
methods for looking ahead. One of those, and the subject of this
book, is that of tea leaf reading (also known as tasseomancy or
tasseography). Many people believe that this practice disappeared
after the Victorian era in England, but that's not true. Tea leaf reading
has continued and is enjoying a resurgence in popularity due to the
growth of both tearooms and spirituality worldwide. Tea leaf reading is the perfect intersection of the simple and the supernatural.

For years, I've performed tea leaf readings for clients in search
of answers. It is one of the many tools in my arsenal as a psychic
medium to help my sitters receive the information they seek.
Unlike tarot (fortune-telling through tarot cards), palmistry
(fortune-telling through hand reading), or scrying (fortune-telling
through crystal balls), tasseomancy is one of the easiest forms of
divination to learn. I was introduced to it by the women in my
family, who performed countless tea leaf readings. Once I tried my
hand at it, it took very little time for me to pick it up. As a conse-
quence, it was one of the first forms I mastered, which is why I'm
excited to offer this book to would-be tea readers and enthusiasts
alike. It's an excellent way to spark your intuition and gain insights

for your friends, family, and yourself. The bonus is you probably have all the tools you need to get started in your kitchen right now!

Why does the unassuming act of sipping tea lend itself to being an excellent form of fortune-telling? Think of how many secrets, tears, and gossip have been shared over a cup of tea. As these conversations take place, the water inside the teacup absorbs energy, and it is a silent witness to all your concerns. When mixed with tea, the energy transforms the shape of tea leaves into familiar images, which if deciphered correctly, hold all the answers you need. Of course, there is a power manipulating those energies to guide you, which I refer to as Spirit. You may call it Source, a Higher Power, or God. All can be used interchangeably.

I am both Romany and a psychic medium, so tea leaf reading is especially near and dear to my heart. Not only did the Romany people help spread this practice, but we firmly put our stamp on it. In fact, every Hollywood movie you have ever seen featuring a tea leaf reader involves a Gypsy stereotype (the term Gypsy is considered a slur and should not be used by non-Romany people). With this book, my goal is not only to teach you about the divinatory art of tasseomancy but also offer a true account of the Romany people and our role within this field. And while we helped popularize this art, it is not exclusive to our culture. Tea leaf reading is not a closed practice. It is open to all those who come to it seeking answers. In fact, my ancestors would love nothing more than to know this beautiful tradition continues to be enjoyed.

At the heart of tea leaf reading is storytelling. Seeming randomness brings together shapes and images via tea leaves and water. It is the reader's job to weave a tale between them. What are the symbols trying to say? Can you find a beginning, middle, and end, all within a few tea clumps in the bottom of a cup? What effect will that message have on the sitter's life?

In my culture, storytelling is an integral part of life. Romany, no matter our variations around the world, can agree on our ability to spin a yarn. We love to interact and share our wisdom and knowledge. Although we are commonly portrayed as an insular people, our joy for others is second to none. Listening to tales around a yog (fire) with laughter, music, good food, and family is a distinct memory from my childhood. The men would frequently play guitars, and while they strummed, the women would sing. And in between, people always took turns telling stories. Many of the stories were filled with laughs, a few were cautionary tales, and some came with tears, but all were entertaining.

Before you is a golden opportunity to become a reader of the leaves and a storyteller of the symbols. I have structured this book so that you can learn the process step by step, each chapter building upon the next. We first look at the history of tea leaf reading in chapter 1. Then, in chapter 2, it's time to get started gathering all the necessary tools and finding out what each does. You'll also begin the ritual of brewing and drinking tea. In chapter 3, you learn how to perform the reading. Chapter 4 provides an extensive glossary of over one hundred symbols to reference during your readings, and chapter 5 offers three example readings to boost your skills. Last, chapter 6 gives you even more options for your newfound skills.

So, let this serve as my invitation to you. I've saved a spot for you by the fire. Come, have a seat, and acquire all the skills needed to go from brewing a cup of tea to utilizing its inner wisdom. Watch your intuition blossom through this beautiful divinatory tool called tea leaf reading. Once you get the hang of it, your skills will only grow from there. Imagine all the hopeful messages you'll be able to give.

CHAPTER 1

THE HISTORY OF TEA LEAF READING

THE ORIGINS OF tea itself began in China and date back to the third century CE, when fragrant leaves were used as a medicinal drink. From that time on, tea slowly spread throughout the world via trade and became immensely popular. In the seventeenth century, tea arrived on England's shores. The British quickly developed a special fondness for the delicious elixir, and it continues to be a pivotal part of British culture to this day. It was in England that the tea leaf reading we still practice today got its start.

When tea was first introduced, tea bags were not yet invented. So, the tea was brewed using loose leaves, which left a residue in the bottom of the teacups. The transition from enjoying a spot of tea to using it for divinatory purposes was a rather easy one to make, since divining the future from sediment was not a wholly unusual practice. Fortune tellers were already utilizing coffee grounds and wine stains to peer into the future.

Tea leaf reading, or tasseomancy, is taken from the French word *tasse* (cup) and the Greek suffix *mancy* (divination). It is the art of using the symbols formed from the residual tea leaves in a cup to predict possible outcomes for the sitter. Tea leaf reading reached its zenith in popularity during the Victorian era (1837–1901), when tea became available to the middle and lower classes and not merely a drink enjoyed by the upper crust.

By this time, tea leaf readings had become synonymous with the Romany, a diasporic people whose origins are in India and who practiced many divination arts. Who better to peer into a mysterious cup of destiny and pick out the symbols inside than a people who had traveled the world? Truly, we have seen it all. And through every place we have lived, we have learned of the human condition intimately. Although you may think a person in India has nothing in common with someone in England, you would be mistaken. The same issues, trials, troubles, and triumphs play out pretty much the same for everyone. This knowledge, combined with the Romany ability to make sense of the otherwise nonsensical, made them front and center practitioners. The Romany are believed to have aided the spread of tasseomancy by conducting readings in parlors, tearooms, and private residences. Since they traveled extensively, by the middle of the 1800s, the practice was found throughout Europe.

Ironically, the decline in tea leaf reading's popularity began with the introduction of tea bags in 1901. Once the tea was finely cut and bagged, the unique characteristics of the loose leaves were stripped away and replaced with an unreadable substitute. Many people mistakenly think that this is where the history of tea leaf reading ends. However, the practice continued, albeit not as widespread as before, within the metaphysical community. Today, spirituality is becoming more accepted in the mainstream, and tasseomancy is experiencing a renaissance. Many practitioners have found new uses for the age-old divinatory tool, such as psychic and mediumship readings and an aid for self-healing and self-reflection. In our modern world, it is perhaps fitting that help can be found in the tools of the past.

CHAPTER 2

PREPARING THE TEA LEAVES

BEFORE WE LEARN what a reading consists of, a quick vocabulary lesson. The person receiving a reading is the *sitter* or the *client* interchangeably. Also, the person giving the reading is the *reader* or *seer*. I will also refer to people as *individuals, sitters, clients,* or *persons*. If I do reference someone in the singular, I use the words *she* or *her* to keep the language from becoming clumsy.

TOOLS FOR TEA LEAF READING

Now that you know the history of tea leaf reading, let's get started! Whether you are reading for yourself or someone else, the steps that follow are the same. First, gather your tools for the reading. Unlike many other forms of divination, you probably already have these items in your home. You need a teacup, saucer, kettle, and loose-leaf tea leaves. The most important of these is the cup. Any teacup will do, but preferably select one that has a wide, flat base and is completely white inside. This allows for clear interpretations of the symbols without the distraction of designs or colors. Maybe you have a family tea set that you would like to use for sentimental reasons, or you may want to start with the fresh energy of a new tea set. Either way, as long as the cup meets the basic criteria, you are ready. In Romany households, we tend to keep our cups for readings separate from our everyday teacups. This may be a practice that you would also like to observe. Plus, using a designated teacup for readings only adds to its energetic charge over time.

BREWING THE TEA AND EMPTYING THE CUP

Now that you have the cup, prepare and cleanse it before doing a reading. Of course, washing it like you would any piece of dishware is a given, but in matters of divination, it is always a good idea to also clear the tool of any spiritual energy.

STEP 1: With your newly washed cup, take some incense (dragon's blood is my favorite) and use the smoke to cleanse the cup inside and out. Swirl the incense stick inside the cup three times in a circular motion, letting the smoke bathe the interior. Then, run the stick around the outside of the cup three times. You can also simply hold your hand a few inches above the cup and imagine a cleansing white light washing over it, taking away any impurities from the cup and leaving you with a beautiful spiritual instrument. Sage and palo santo can also be used, but be aware of the cultural sensitivities related to these products, such as the cultural appropriation of Indigenous cultures and overharvesting of both plants. If you are in doubt, incense works best.

STEP 2: Now that your cup is both physically and spiritually clean, let's say a few words of encouragement over it. I like to recite this incantation over any new cup I get before putting it into my tea leaf reading rotation. With that, the teacup is ready for use.

Be now a tool of sight,
From leaves of tea in your cup of white,
Help make the message plain,
Of fate and fortune I do proclaim.

STEP 3: To prepare yourself for a reading, try to take a few minutes earlier in the day to meditate to clear your head and ground yourself, but it isn't necessary. My Romany ancestors did not do much in the way of meditating, but they did keep their intentions focused and were not distracted once it was time to do a reading. Intention is key to all psychic endeavors. Once you set the aim for the work you are about to do, it immediately transforms the mundane into the magical.

STEP 4: The next most important step is brewing the tea. Since you are making one cup for one reading, you need only a small amount of tea leaves. In most cases, a pinch of tea leaves will suffice. The most crucial thing to remember is that it needs to be loose leaf. Bagged teas are too fine and do not have enough character to read. Black, green, and oolong loose-leaf teas are the most common teas used for readings. For a beginner, simple black loose-leaf tea works best.

STEP 5: Since we're using tea for divinatory purposes, brew it in a kettle. Heat the water as you normally would to prepare tea.

(It tastes better that way to me anyway.) Add a pinch or up to a ½ teaspoon of loose-leaf tea directly into the teacup. When the kettle sounds, pour the piping-hot water into the cup. Let it steep for three to five minutes.

STEP 6: While the tea steeps, take a few moments to prepare the space in which the reading will take place. Again, you can use incense with its cleansing smoke to clear the energies before a reading. You can also say a few words to invite your guides, angels, and ancestors in to preside over the reading and to help you channel the information coming through.

STEP 7: With the tea ready and your space and mind clear, it is time to drink. Traditionally, the tea is drank straight up. No milk, no sugar, and no chasers. Again, this is a ceremony and not a treat, so keep that in mind. The sitter may now begin drinking the tea (or you if conducting a self-reading). However, if you're reading for a friend or paying client, sometimes it is not possible for her to drink the tea, as you may be conducting the reading via phone or online. In such cases, you can drink the tea for the client and sit in as her proxy. Additionally, if the sitter is in the same room as you but isn't a fan of tea or has other needs that you would like to accommodate, have the sitter swish the cup around a few times, as her essence can be read without any problems.

STEP 8: Before taking the first sip, reflect on a question you would like answered (or have the sitter reflect on a question if reading for another person). Conversely, if there is no particular issue at hand, you can let your mind wander freely while sipping away. The same goes when you read for someone else. The solutions will come forth regardless. That is the intelligence of Spirit. While drinking the tea, take as much time as desired. No need to rush this moment.

STEP 9: When almost all the liquid is gone, or about ½ teaspoon remains, it is time to begin conducting the actual reading. This part is important, as too much remaining liquid will simply wash away all the tea leaves onto the saucer with nothing in the cup left to read.

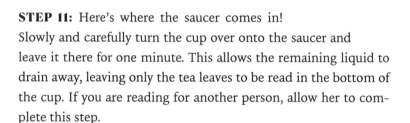

STEP 10: Take the cup by the handle using your left hand. With the cup facing upward, swirl the remaining tea leaves and liquid around three times in a counterclockwise circle, left to right.

STEP 11: Here's where the saucer comes in! Slowly and carefully turn the cup over onto the saucer and leave it there for one minute. This allows the remaining liquid to drain away, leaving only the tea leaves to be read in the bottom of the cup. If you are reading for another person, allow her to complete this step.

STEP 12: Once the time has elapsed, turn the cup upright. You will see the tea leaves have formed into clumps and clusters of various sizes and shapes in the bottom of the cup. This is where all the magic lives!

UNDERSTANDING THE TEACUP LAYOUT

So, now you are staring at the tea leaves and a slight panic may race up your spine. Maybe you are thinking, *Yikes! What did I get myself into?* No need to worry. Take a deep breath. You got this. We'll begin with some basic anatomy to orient you to the teacup before interpreting the symbols. This will give an idea of how it relates to the reading before you.

The Teacup's Handle

The most important piece is the teacup's handle. This represents the person receiving the reading. If a tea leaf symbol is found close to the handle, its impact on the sitter is greater. If it's farther away from the handle, a symbol's influence on the sitter is lessened. The handle is also a great starting point for the reading. From here, you can work around the cup in a clockwise fashion while reading the

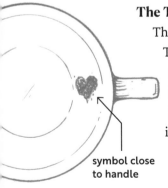

symbol close
to handle

symbols, starting with the rim and moving down the cup. Because you use the teacup's handle as a starting point and the cup is turned in a clockwise fashion, this causes the symbols to appear differently oriented within the cup. The key is to go with the image as it first appears to you.

The Teacup's Rim

The outer rim of the teacup represents the near future, up to no more than a month out. As you move farther inside the cup, you move further into the future. The middle section represents anywhere from a month to several months out, while the very center (bottom) denotes the furthest timeline, up to a year away. With tasseomancy, the cup provides a beautiful arrangement for timing.

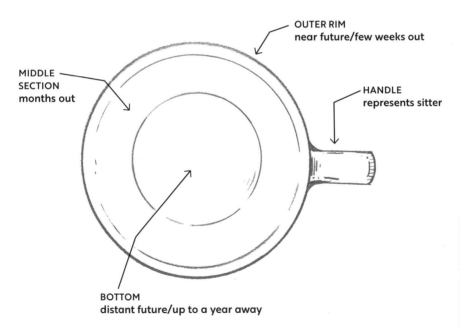

OUTER RIM
near future/few weeks out

MIDDLE
SECTION
months out

HANDLE
represents sitter

BOTTOM
distant future/up to a year away

INTERPRETING
TEA LEAF SYMBOLS

NOW THAT YOU'RE familiar with the layout of the teacup and it's teeming with symbols, let's get to the best part—interpreting the tea leaf symbols! Which symbols pop out first? How do they relate to one another? What is the overall message of the cup? Follow these simple steps to find out!

make note of
first symbols seen

STEP 1: Working from the handle in a clockwise motion, let your gaze be soft and your mind receptive. You can simply let your eyes move around the cup, noting any symbols that appear, but most readers pick up the cup and rotate it to get a closer look at its contents. Once you've spotted a symbol, continue rotating the cup to ensure none are missed. The key here is going with what catches your eye first. If the initial symbol you see is a dragon (page 65), note it. Trust me that is going to be important.

STEP 2: As you turn the cup one full rotation, stop to take note of what you have seen. You may want to have a piece of paper and pen handy and jot down the images as they come to you. Keep in mind that not every tiny tea leaf needs to be scrutinized. Stick with the ones that jump out at you.

STEP 3: As you're doing your initial survey of the cup, explain what you are seeing and allow the sitter to offer feedback if performing for another person. After your first once-over, you may want to do another pass or two, as the smaller symbols will help fill in any blanks. Again, it is all going to work out just as it needs to. Weave the tale of the teacup. Be its storyteller. It is literally all in your hands.

For humans, imagination and intuition reside in the same space. Do not hold yourself back from what you interpret. Do not be self-conscious about conveying what you see. With time, you will find you worry less and less about how something sounds and will trust that each symbol, no matter how odd, was placed there on purpose. Each of us has specific attributes that make us the unique individuals we are. Spirit knows this. Perhaps you love to knit or collect cat figurines. Spirit can use the knowledge you already possess to help you decode the reading and give an accurate message.

There is a mantra I use that you are welcome to try until you have been doing this for a while. It goes like this: *What I see is meant for me.* The meaning is that you and I may look into the same cup and not necessarily see the same things. What catches the eye first may be different for each of us, which is okay and exactly how it should be. When you read tea leaves, what you see is meant for only you to see, understand, and interpret. The client will receive the precise message she is supposed to. That is how the intelligence of Spirit works. They know just what symbols to choose in order to get their message across.

Tea leaf reading is not an exact science. It is an art form. It takes time and requires the three Ps: patience, peace of mind, and persistence. Equip yourself with those and you will get the hang of it in no time. Do not come to a reading with any assumptions. Do not try to anticipate what is going to appear in the teacup. Try to keep your mind as clear as possible. It is not much different than a Rorschach test of ink blot tests that psychiatrists use. Humans love to make pictures out of almost anything. While this may seem coincidental or just imagination, it is the beauty of how Spirit works. You do not have to be a walking encyclopedia of spiritual information. You only need to be yourself. Spirit will use the information already in your brain to help you decipher the message.

TEA LEAF LAWS

Regardless of which symbols appear in the cup, all of them have four distinct characteristics to keep in mind: (1) location, (2) appearance, (3) way, and (4) size. *Location* relates to where the symbol is within the cup, which we have already covered (page 15). *Appearance* refers to how clear the symbol is—does it look distinctly like a symbol or vaguely like a symbol? *Way* is the direction in which the symbol is pointing: toward the handle or away. And lastly, *size* relates to how big or small a symbol is. I've adopted a mnemonic device—LAWS— to keep these in mind. As in everyday life, remembering to obey laws makes life a bit easier. As long as you practice these tea leaf reading LAWS, you will be set for success!

Let's look at the symbol of a knife to illustrate how each characteristic plays an integral part in defining a symbol's meaning. A knife within the teacup is a warning of trouble ahead (page 86). Based on the LAWS, we can determine when this might occur, what type of trouble it is, who it will affect, and how much trouble it might turn out to be.

Location

The location of a symbol within the cup helps determine timing. The closer to the rim, the shorter the amount of time there is before events unfold. The farther away from the rim—toward the bottom of the cup—you go, the further the timeline gets pushed out. The normal rule for timing is that the rim represents the near future, within a few days to weeks. The middle of the cup represents several months away, and the bottom of the cup represents about a year out.

Checking the location of the knife within the teacup helps determine when it will take place. In the first image below, the knife is sitting on the rim of the cup. This would indicate trouble for the sitter is likely to happen within a short time period, no longer than a couple of weeks. However, in the second image, the knife is found at the bottom of the cup. In this case, the trouble could still be several months to a year away. Knowing the timing of an event gives the sitter options when it comes to coping with a potential situation.

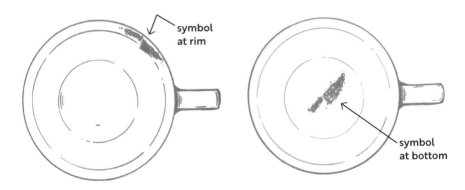

symbol at rim

symbol at bottom

Appearance

For appearance, the clarity of the symbol matters a great deal. If a symbol is distinct and easy to make out, its meaning usually has a more positive connotation. The more defined a symbol is the easier it is to determine its meaning with little ambiguity. However, if the symbol is cloudy or murky, the tone of the omen changes, usually becoming more negative in meaning.

Again, using the knife as an example, the first image shows it clearly defined and outlined. There is no doubt that is a knife. When it appears this way, the meaning becomes crystal clear as well. Something unpleasant *is* going to happen. On the other hand, the second image shows a fuzzy knife. This casts doubt as to whether the trouble will come to pass or not. For example, the sitter may indeed have a false friend spreading gossip about her, but no one ends up believing it, and no real damage is caused to the sitter.

clear image   fuzzy symbol

Way

The direction in which the symbol is oriented is also important. The way in which the symbol lies in relationship to the handle represents the impact to the sitter. If the symbol points to or faces the handle, the situation at hand is happening *to* the sitter. However, if it is facing away from the handle, the sitter is much more in control of the unfolding events.

Going back to our trusty knife symbol, in the first image, it points directly at the cup's handle. This indicates the sitter is going to be on the receiving end of future trouble. But in the second image, the knife is pointing away from the handle. In this case, the sitter has the upper hand, and she will possibly be the one inflicting a little trouble of her own.

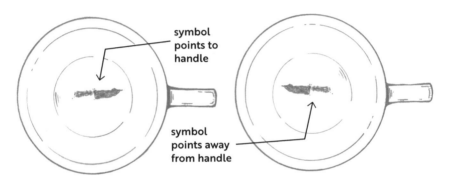

symbol points to handle

symbol points away from handle

Size

Finally, the size of the symbol represents its power. The bigger the symbol, the bigger its effect and vice versa. Due to size, a negative symbol's impact can be lessened if it is small, and a positive symbol's impact can be strengthened if it is large. To determine whether a symbol is large or small, look at the other symbols in the cup and judge their size relative to one another.

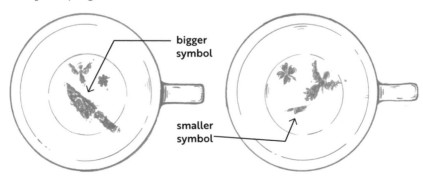

bigger symbol

smaller symbol

In the first image, the knife is the biggest symbol in the tea-cup. As such, while there are other mitigating symbols in the form of an angel (page 34) and four-leaf clover (page 58), trouble will be affecting the sitter. In the second image, the sitter has a much better chance of not experiencing this trouble at all, as the knife is much smaller than the angel and four-leaf clover.

TEA LEAF SYMBOL FORMATIONS

A few symbols within tea leaf reading not only have their own meanings, but when found in certain formations, can help strengthen surrounding symbols. For example, a *triangle* (page 119) found by itself means unexpected good fortune. However, if another symbol appears within the triangle, it will enhance the other symbol's meaning. A *bee* (page 40) indicates a busy time or success at work. When found within a triangle, it will be even more busy or successful for the sitter. In the case of *dots*, they need to be associated with another symbol in order to be given specific meaning, as they are quite common to see in any given tea leaf reading. If you find dots surrounding another symbol, either partially or completely, then make note of that as they will be intensifying the symbol's meaning, whether positive or negative. All these enhancing symbols are found within the following glossary and are as follows: circle, dots, lines, square, and triangle. As always, make note of each symbol's meaning to combine them into one cohesive reading.

triangle symbol by itself

additional symbol inside a triangle

READING TEA LEAVES
FOR YOURSELF AND OTHERS

Finally, let's differentiate between reading for yourself and reading for others. When you read for yourself, there is not as much pressure to perform. The symbols will appear in the cup. It is your job to look at them and interpret their meanings. It is somewhat stress-free because you are, of course, aware of what is going on in your life. The story tends to come together more easily due to this fact.

When reading for someone else, remember that you are merely the channel through which Spirit is speaking. You did not place the symbols in the cup. You have not manipulated anything to make it come out as you want. Remind sitters that their future is always in flux. Free will rules the Universe. So, one small decision, and everything unwinds and forms into quite another picture altogether. Any type of psychic reading is merely a snapshot of the sitter's life at that moment in time. It is not set in stone. Heck, it is not even set in the leaves! Things can and often do change. What is great about a tea leaf reading—even a "bad" one—is that it gives the sitter a heads-up about what to look out for. The simple act of having the reading could prompt the sitter to head off mistakes that would otherwise turn into disasters. It may prompt a sitter to make different decisions. Or it may confirm that she is on the right path.

But the most important thing to avoid is putting too much pressure on yourself. Practicing divination can have serious undertones, but at its heart, it is a fun way to tap into your intuition. You are simply having a cup of tea and letting the secrets spill forth.

TRICKS OF THE TRADE

Over the years, I have picked up some helpful tips and tricks I'd like to share with you. Keep these handy as you're reading. They may help you out of a sticky situation or answer a question that pops up in the course of your practice. Also, jot down useful tidbits you learn along the way and compile your tricks of the trade!

✦ Sometimes through the course of a reading you may introduce a new concept to your client. A great example of this is manifesting. It is very popular in spiritual and non-spiritual circles alike. If you ever spot a wand in the teacup, the timing is perfect for manifesting. Manifestation is the act of bringing something into your life through focused intention and inspired action. Manifesting may be a new concept to sitters, and they may ask how to get started. While the topic is extensive, this simple advice can be offered. Imagine something you want. With that image in mind, let yourself feel as if it has already happened. It is key to become emotionally connected to the outcome you seek. Be open to letting the Universe work out the details of how it comes to be. Simply keep the intention's focus by repeating the exercise daily, either through visualization or making a mantra of it. Most importantly, offer gratitude for the eventual results the Universe will provide.

✦ Understanding what each symbol means is important, but as seer, you must also take the full picture of what you find in the teacup into account. Throughout the following glossary, you will find both negative and positive symbols that reflect life. We face both the good and the bad throughout our journeys here on earth. Before growing concerned by a negative or bad sign that pops out at you, survey the entire scene. You may soon realize that the good omens outweigh the bad. That is why it is important to take your time before beginning a reading. Let the picture fully come into focus before you give any dire warnings or misgivings to yourself or the sitter. This prevents any undue stress and unnecessary embarrassment.

✦ Always advise a sitter that you **cannot** and **will not** provide medical diagnoses. Encourage the sitter to seek the counsel of a medical professional for all health-related issues.

✦ If you decide to take up tasseomancy as a professional reader, it is always a good idea to have contact information for domestic or sexual abuse hotlines and shelters on hand in case the client needs it. Many times, clients will tell readers information that they would never tell anyone else. It is a moral and ethical imperative to be responsible with that information and offer tools to clients when needed.

✦ Never place personal judgments on the client's situation. Each of us is on our own journey. As a reader, it is your job to decipher the message, not deliver opinions.

✦ Make it a priority never to frighten your sitter. There are some symbols that carry a more negative connotation, but taken in its totality, rarely is an entire reading negative. Never insinuate the sitter is somehow evil or a bad person simply because the tone of the reading may not be as light and airy as you would prefer. Never, ever intimate that a sitter has a negative attachment or entity connected to her or that her negative karma has caused all her issues. Stay out of the judgment game and your readings will go much more smoothly.

✦ Do not take an isolated symbol and spell doom and gloom for the sitter. Words matter, especially for a reader. It is vitally important to consider your words before uttering them. Whether reading tea leaves for fun or professionally, be mindful that what is said during any psychic reading has an impact on sitters. There is a moral obligation by anyone performing spiritual arts to take into account potential damage that can be caused by being careless with one's words. You may only ever read for yourself or friends, but do not discount how much weight a glimpse into the future can have on others.

✦ Trust that the information showing up for you is exactly what the sitter needs to hear. Spirit uses all your life experiences and information contained within your aura to get their message across. So, the symbols you see within the teacup are going to be the perfect references for you to give just the right message. That is the intelligence of Spirit, and it will not let you down.

✦ One last word about conducting readings. If the tea leaves within the cup appear severely muddled or your head is fuzzy and unclear of how to make heads or tails of what is in the cup, it is perfectly acceptable, nay entirely responsible of you, to postpone the reading until the conditions seem more favorable. Better to delay a reading than give an incomplete or inaccurate one.

CHAPTER 4

TEA LEAF SYMBOL GLOSSARY

T HE FOLLOWING GLOSSARY is a beginner's guide into the world of tea leaf reading symbology. There are more than one hundred symbols listed here. Obviously, it does not include each and every tea leaf symbol you may come across while conducting a reading, but it is a starter set that you can add to as you begin conducting readings. The meanings of the symbols are derived from what I've come to know throughout my years of practice, as well as the knowledge of many other tea leaf readers out there. However, I truly encourage you to insert your meanings if these do not feel right to you. I want this book to encourage you to trust your intuition and psychic abilities. Remember my earlier mantra: *What I see is meant for me.* This goes for the tea leaf symbol meanings as well. I am not advising you to go be willy-nilly and abandon these tried-and-true meanings, but do allow yourself to trust your inner wisdom. Soon you will have a personal glossary that is a mix of these meanings and your developed personal knowledge.

ACORN

Better times ahead, coming riches, restored health

When found in a teacup, the tiny fruit of the mighty oak tree is a fortuitous sign indeed. An acorn is a seed that holds the hope of a new beginning for its species. But when acorns fall, they come to settle beneath the dark shadows of towering trees. However, it is in this darkness that the chance for renewal springs forth. Similarly, in a reading, an acorn represents growth and better times coming in one's life. The sitter most likely is dealing with challenges at present, but with this symbol, assurance is offered that things will be improving soon.

Alternatively, abundance may await the client. Think of the busy squirrel gathering up all the acorns he can find before the cold winter. Once the bitter winds and snow hit, the squirrel is snuggled warmly in his tree, munching away on his store. For the sitter, extra money or other resources may be on the way. This might be in the form of a raise, job change, or investments paying off. Chances of lottery winnings or windfalls are also possible, but more likely the extra income will come from the client's effort, much like the industrious squirrel. Keep in mind that if the acorn is bigger than the surrounding symbols, the increase will be substantial. If it is much smaller, then it might be a temporary surplus only. An acorn is also a great sign that an improvement in health is likely.

TIP As a reminder, encourage the sitter to seek a medical professional's opinion for all health-related matters.

AIRPLANE

Long distance journey, quick trip

Who doesn't love a trip away? When this symbol appears in a reading, it predicts a journey of great distances, most likely overseas or at least cross-country. Perhaps an important trip is coming up for the sitter or an exotic vacation beckons. If the sitter claims no travel plans to date, then this will definitely be enlightening information. Based on the location within the cup, the timing of this journey can be determined. If the airplane is found near the rim, the trip will be happening in the near future, within a few days to weeks. If it is located in the middle, the trip will be further out, up to several months away. And if it is at the bottom, the sitter will have time to plan, as it might not happen until a year out.

Although the distance may be great, the length of this trip is usually short. So, no month-long stays in the Serengeti in Tanzania, but a down-and-dirty dash to Mallorca, Spain, may do the trick. This can be for either business or personal reasons. Surrounding symbols will reveal more details. For example, if the airplane is found alongside a ring (page 106) and/or bells (page 41), then a destination wedding could be on the horizon.

Leave room for a more straightforward interpretation with this symbol. Seeing an airplane could be in reference to a future or current career for the sitter (e.g., pilot, flight attendant, or mechanic). Again, neighboring symbols will guide the meaning.

ALLIGATOR

Betrayal, rivalry

Alligators are natural villains. They swim beneath the water, with most of their bodies hidden while only their eyes remain visible. About the time prey realizes what is happening, it is already too late. As these animals are known for snapping up unsuspecting victims, the same holds true when finding their likeness within the teacup. Betrayal may be afoot. There is possibly a traitor among the sitter's friends. Just as the alligator does not show all of himself all at once, the same could be said of some of the sitter's friends or family members. And when these revelations are made, it is tough to hear. These people are usually those closest to someone, making that disloyalty all the more painful. Look for additional symbols, such as a bat (page 38) or knife (page 86), which would bolster the interpretation that someone within the sitter's life is not being honest. This could point to an upcoming heartache within the sitter's romantic relationship. As always, be thorough in getting the full picture before drawing any conclusions.

An alligator can also represent a rival in the client's life. Ever come to a stoplight, and when the light turns green, the other driver peels off and you realize you were in race you never agreed to? The same applies here. The client may have knowledge of this rival or it may come as a surprise. This can be in a work environment or a personal matter as well. Depending on the nearby symbols, what to do about this rivalry, if anything, can be determined.

ANCHOR

Stability, success in love/business, putting down roots

Dropping anchor means a destination has been reached. It is time to secure the boat in place for safety's sake. So it is with the anchor symbol. No more being tossed about on the open sea. The sitter's life will soon become much more stable. The anchor signifies that moment when the extreme highs and lows of life reach an even keel, bringing with it much-needed relief.

Additionally, when an anchor appears in a reading, success is assured, especially in the areas of love or business. A resounding yes to the question of a business idea taking off or if a budding romance is destined for the long run. Check for clarity in the omen. The more defined the anchor, the greater the achievement. If it is cloudy or jumbled in appearance, more work may need to be done before the accomplishment is realized.

This can also be a good sign for settling down. The client may have inquired as to whether the purchase of a new home is possible or if starting a family can happen soon. The chances of either are pretty good when the anchor appears. It is all about reaching that place of contentment and wanting to merge with the good feeling it arouses within you. Who doesn't want to sink their roots into that?

ANGEL

Good news, protection

Regardless of religious background, most agree that angels are guardians, protectors, and messengers from Spirit. And that is exactly what an angel represents in the tea leaves. Maybe the sitter wants to know if a loan will get approved. This symbol points to yes! Will little Susie get into that Ivy League college? No question. Remember, this information can reach the sitter in many ways. The message may come through snail mail, email, text, or even DMs. Trust me, Spirit keeps up with the times. The most important part is the news will be good.

Besides playing the role of messenger, angels have also been known to serve and protect. During the reading with an angel in the leaves, look to the nearby symbols to determine whether the angel means good news or protection. It can be both. At times, sensitive situations can be touched upon in readings, such as domestic violence or sexual abuse. In this context, Spirit is advising that the sitter needs protection. The spiritual version via an angel is already given, but more needs to be done in the physical to ensure the sitter's safety.

TIP Just a reminder that clients may disclose information to you that they haven't told anyone else. Take that responsibility seriously. If within the course of a reading you realize she may need some help, it's always a good idea to provide them with a resource to reach out to.

ARROW

Message coming, direction of life progress

This one is pretty straightforward . . . or should I say backward, up, or down? An arrow, regardless of which way it is facing, indicates an incoming message. Unfortunately, this is not as cut and dry as the previous angel omen. The news here might be good *or* bad. In this case, take into account the full layout of the cup. If the arrow is accompanied by a blurry feather (page 69), snake (page 110), or bear (page 39), the news will not be great. On the other hand, paired with the angel (page 34), a deer (page 61), and a distinct feather (page 69), pop the Champagne! Again, the future is fluid. So, equipped with this newly acquired information, the sitter may make a different decision and avoid the bad news all together.

In addition, an arrow can be an indication of what direction the client's life is taking. If pointing up, things are going well. If straight down, not so much. Left or right requires a little more nuance to determine. Possibly the client wants to know if a partner is the right one or not. If so and the arrow is pointing to the right, I would interpret that as a yes. Remember, imagination and intuition are separated by only a few letters. Use them in tandem and discerning the leaves will come much more easily.

AXE

Resentment, "axe to grind," overcoming adversity

Ever attain a new level in life or accomplish something big and there is that one friend who seems not so excited about it? Maybe doubts creep in that this person resents the success. But in polite society, that thought is pushed away. Sorry to say, but this symbol in the tea leaves means someone is definitely resentful. No one ever wants to think they could have secret enemies, but alas, the world is not as ideal as we would like it to be. If the sitter seems stumped about who this could be, look to the accompanying symbols. Are there any letters? The tea leaves frequently put out enough information to give a complete answer.

Sometimes the resentment can turn to an all-out grudge. When seeing an axe in the cup, pay attention to which way it is pointing. Direction is important. If the blade lies toward the handle, it could indicate the danger from this person's treachery is closer than it appears. If turned away, there may be a tough time caused by this person, but ultimately the client will overcome it.

Speaking of overcoming, this is also a sign of facing adversity but coming out on top. When seeing an axe, more times than not, the client is familiar with this troublemaker. In fact, the impetus for the reading might be figuring out what to do about this person. In my experience, this at least gives the client confirmation that her suspicions are correct and can empower her to take the necessary steps to draw boundaries with this person and take care of the issue. As always, information is power.

BASKET

New addition to the family, gift

Babies and baskets go all the way back to the time of Moses. Traditionally, babies slept in baskets, ensuring a close connection with their mother. With that in mind, a basket formed within the tea leaves indicates a new addition to the family. Perhaps the sitter has gone through fertility difficulties and is hoping for a successful pregnancy. This symbol would be encouraging in that instance. Again, always look to the surrounding symbols. But if there were also a rainbow and an angel (page 34) in the cup, I would be tempted to send the birth announcements myself. New babies do include both the human and fur variety. Maybe the sitter is hoping a pet adoption will go through. This would be a clear yes as well. Beyond babies, in-laws are also additional family members. So, if the sitter assures you that babies are not a consideration, a wedding might be upcoming.

In the case where neither babies nor in-laws are being added, a basket can also indicate a gift, usually given by someone new to the sitter's life. Maybe a recent addition to the office wants to thank the sitter for showing them the ropes and will send a gift as a show of appreciation.

TIP Remember that any psychic reading captures only a moment in time. Life is always in flux. So, if the client freaks out at the mention of babies, advise that this can also be Spirit's way of offering a heads-up so that a different choice can be made. I always phrase it this way: *I see that there is a new addition possible to your family. If you are not looking to add children at this time, take the necessary precautions.* It is simple and effective.

BAT

False friends, fruitless undertakings, stuck in place

When a bat swoops into the cup, the sitter may want to keep their eyes peeled for any people acting strangely. It does not feel good to doubt those closest to you. Sometimes, life takes a turn and those who once were close friends grow apart. This situation is not as serious as the axe (page 36). The person or persons are not out to get the sitter per se, but they may be spreading idle gossip and not providing an otherwise safe space.

If more positive symbols surround the bat than negative ones, the meaning can change slightly. In this case, the bat represents wasted energy or potential. It could be the client has started a business or hobby that is not cut out for the long haul. It may be taking more time and energy than it is giving back in resources and fun. This is one of those symbols to break gently to the client. No one wants to be told that something is a waste of time. A more diplomatic approach would be to explain it is probable a current venture had great intentions, but it doesn't seem to be panning out and the sitter may want to take a look at areas of life that could use some recalibrating. Because, ultimately, if the sitter continues to stay in an unproductive situation, this energy suck becomes much more of a problem. The sitter may start to feel stuck in place. Life can feel a little upside down. If the sitter acknowledges this is the current situation, then look to neighboring symbols to see if the situation will be easing soon.

BEAR

Obstacles or risks based on bad decisions, mama bear energy

Bears are awesome creatures indeed, fiercely protective and capable of much destruction. Most humans avoid them at all costs. Who wants to tangle with five hundred pounds of sharp teeth and claws? Not me. But humans make mistakes. We wander off the beaten path and right into a sleeping bear's cave. Oopsie. In this scenario, we unknowingly got ourselves into a bad situation. But at other times, we walk right into that bear cave and poke it with a stick. Seeing a bear in the tea leaves represents a risk caused by the sitter's bad decisions. This can be a hard symbol to relay to the sitter because it requires taking responsibility for one's actions. It is likely the sitter is dealing with an obstacle because of past choices. This is not the time to play the blame game. Simply look to the other symbols for the full story and gently advise that this is a learning experience.

A different meaning for this omen is that of mama bear energy. This can represent the client or someone in the client's life. There could be an issue regarding the client's children, causing the client to be on high alert. Ask any mother what lengths she is willing to go to if someone threatens her children and you will understand the client's current state. Here the nearby symbols will help paint a clear picture of the issues forcing the mama bear out of her cave and into harm's way to protect what she loves.

BEE

Busy time, success at work

Ever busy and productive, the bee is the bastion of work life. When the bee appears in a teacup, the sitter is entering an industrious time, most likely at work. The sitter may be in a building phase or entering a new position, which requires a few extra hours and elbow grease to reach the goals at hand. But those goals will be met, and others will take note of the sitter's hard work. The bee tends to show up when the sitter is hitting a peak in her career or training. It is that moment just before everything comes together, but it feels like it is just about to fall apart. The sitter might have too much on her plate and is being warned of burnout. The surrounding symbols will reveal the full meaning.

Due to productivity during this busy time, success is most assured. The client may be a budding fashion designer, spending late nights in the studio, surviving on little more than caffeine and hope. Then, that daring fashionista seeks out a tea leaf reading. There sits a bee in the cup calling out to the sitter to hang in there and keep hustling because all this hard work will not be in vain.

BELL

Announcement, happy news, positive changes

Long before the ding of app notifications, bells were the method used to announce breaking news to the neighboring community, usually ringing from the local church. We still use bells as a method of alert, starting with the telephone, although now our ringtones are much more expressive. The sitter may soon have news to share when this symbol pops up in the teacup. It could be a wedding or baby announcement. Whatever the topic of announcement, it will be a great bit of news and worthy of sharing with family and friends alike.

The bell is also a symbol for receiving good news. The news may be about almost any area of life and it could be received myriad ways. Depending on the nearby symbols, when a bell appears in the tea leaves, it can also proclaim positive changes for the client. It could be the client has dealt with some hard times recently, and the bells have shown up to let her know things will get better. Apply the LAWS (page 19) to this symbol, and the timing and amount of change may be ascertained.

BROOM

New home, life changes, clearing away debris

Time to welcome a new season into the sitter's life. A broom (or besom) indicates the purchase of a new home. There is an old practice of buying a broom when moving into a new home. It is said to bring good luck. Leaving an old broom at the last residence keeps the dirt/energy from the previous house from following the owner. In the teacup, if the broom is found near the rim, this move will take place soon. Toward the middle of the cup, the move should occur within the next several months, and at the bottom of the cup, the move could still be around a year away.

If the client has no intentions of purchasing a new home at this time, life changes in general are being referenced by this symbol. This could be a moment of transition in the client's life. I have found a broom to show up in a reading when the sitter has just gone through a major event, such as a divorce, wedding, childbirth, job change, or death in the family. Something about these crucial moments leads us all to re-evaluate and re-examine our goals and dreams. It is usually followed by a great period of self-growth for the client. So, while change can be scary, ultimately it should be embraced.

The broom also stands for a chance at fresh energy and clearing away stagnant feelings. Time to declutter in the sitter's home and possibly mind. A broom is a simple but powerful tool. With each swish, a clean surface is exposed. The sitter may very well be in the middle of a healing journey, and this is a great sign to continue in that direction. Healing is taking place!

BIRDS

News (single bird), good news (if flying),
delay (if standing), travel

Birds have always been used as messengers, well before the first tweet was sent. Pigeons carried messages in ancient Greece and Rome. For the most part, birds that appear in the tea leaves are good signs. If there is only one, it simply means news is on the way. Neighboring symbols can help decipher whether its nature is good or bad. If the bird seems to be in flight, the news is assuredly good. However, if the bird appears to be standing still or perched, there might be a delay in the sitter's current plans.

Because birds do travel long distances, sometimes migrating thousands of miles, seeing them in a reading is a sign of upcoming travel. If accompanied by a boat (page 44) or horse (page 79) in the tea leaves, then the sitter should already have bags packed!

Using the LAWS (page 19) can help determine more details about this otherwise unimpressive omen. What is the location of the bird(s) within the cup? This will determine when the sitter can expect this news. How's the appearance? Are the birds clearly delineated or fuzzy? This will indicate whether the news is positive or not. Which way are the birds facing? If they are looking toward the handle, the sitter will receive this news. But if the birds are flying away from the handle, perhaps the sitter has news to deliver to someone else. Finally, what size are the birds in relation to the nearby symbols? The bigger they appear, the more important the news will be.

BOAT

Friend will visit, possible journey, ship has come in

When a boat pops up, a friend will, too. Use additional symbols to determine whether this is a visit from a friend or someone who is a little more than a friend. It is possible the sitter is in need of some support at this time. I have always found friends show up right at the perfect time when that is the case.

Keep in mind that many of the symbols found in tea leaf readings have been in use for at least a couple of centuries now, and times change. While having an unexpected house guest may have once been the routine and even preferred method of visiting with a friend, now most folks catch up over a cup of coffee or even a text. So, understand that although the practice of tea leaf reading has been around for a long time, it is able to adapt and be modified to the current day.

Finding a boat in the leaves can also mean the client may not be receiving guests but rather getting ready to go on a journey instead. This could be that once-in-a-lifetime cruise or a fishing expedition that the client has always dreamed of. Most likely, it is a physical journey and not a metaphorical one, but as always, apply the surrounding symbols to get the full story.

Last, this symbol can indicate an achievement. Is the client up for a promotion? Maybe the client recently thought of starting a business and is toying with the idea, but she is unsure of taking the leap. If there are more positive symbols within the cup, such as the sun (page 115), I would encourage the client to get started with it right away.

BRIDGE

Leads to someone/somewhere, way out of problems,
movement in life

Bridges help make connections. They move us from point A to B, usually over precarious waters or heights. Within the tea leaves, a bridge offers a similar solution. First, the bridge may be leading the sitter to a new someone or somewhere in life. Coming after a recent breakup or job loss, a bridge would bring a joyful change of pace. It portends new opportunities at work, at home, and in love. The bridge also frequently shows up when the sitter is dealing with a broken friendship. This signifies that there will be a reunion between the two parties.

Similarly, the client might be super stressed. Bills are piling up, work is demanding, and life is simply chaotic. These readings usually revolve around the question: "Will things ever get better?" Thankfully, when a bridge appears, the answer is a great big yes! With this particular symbol, I always find myself referencing the song, "A Bridge over Troubled Water." As intimated in the song, the sitter is receiving the promise of safe passage over turbulent times. It is a sign of hope that things will indeed get better.

Overall, the bridge symbolizes positive movement within the client's life. When someone is struggling and life is overwhelming, it can feel like it has been that way for a long time. The client may feel stuck and mired in the problems, but the bridge transports the client from current problems into future possibilities.

BREAD

Nourishment, well-being, taking care of one's self

What is better than a warm loaf of bread with some melted butter? Not much. Breadmaking practically became a national pastime during 2020. It is one of those rare foods that can both sustain and soothe us all at once—something we were all in dire need of during that uncertain time. When bread is found in the cup, symbolically speaking, consider offering this advice to the sitter: time for some self-care. It could be that the sitter is in short supply of a little TLC and needs this encouragement to proceed. Maybe the sitter has already begun incorporating self-care into her routine and Spirit wants to recognize that.

This omen tends to show up for those who always put others first. Caretakers, mothers, teachers, nurses . . . the list is long. It is second nature to these individuals to comfort and care for others. Not a moment's hesitation is given when asked to sacrifice their own needs. However, they would never consider taking a day off, getting a massage, or being pampered in any way, until they receive a tea leaf reading and Spirit lays it all out for them. Explain that when they take time to recharge their batteries, they can continue being the best version of themselves for all those who count on them. It is all a matter of perspective.

BUTTERFLY

Lucky/worry-free period, soul, frivolity/vanity

Butterflies are one of the most exquisite examples of metamorphosis. They evoke a sense of wonder that most cannot deny when they drift into view. Since butterflies can represent so many stages of transformation, they carry a few different meanings within the tea leaves.

First, it is lucky to find a butterfly in the cup. The sitter will move into a period of ease. Much like the gentle butterfly, troubles will be light. Burdens will lift from the sitter's shoulders. If debts or drama have been plaguing the sitter, this omen will bring about a much-needed respite from those issues.

Secondly, the butterfly represents the soul. Spirit loves to use butterflies to let loved ones know they are near. When one is found inside the teacup, this reading could turn a little mediumistic. This symbol may be used by a loved one to say hello or a guide is popping in. Use this meaning if the sitter has inquired about relatives who have crossed over or if a question comes up regarding messages from guides.

Sometimes a butterfly can represent floating and gliding through life without much structure or planning. The client may feel listless or without direction at the current time. This serves as a gentle warning that some responsibility needs to be taken to course correct. While a lax approach may be necessary at times, getting too lost in the moment may cause a loss in focus on bigger issues at hand.

CANDLE

Hope, person who helps others

A candle, although equipped with only a small flame, can fill an entire room. A light in the darkness beckons those who need help to follow it. The sitter may be badly in need of a little optimism at this time. And with this symbol, Spirit is bringing it. When a candle shows up in the leaves, hope is on the way. This symbol frequently shows up when a sitter may be at the end of her rope. I have had many clients ready to throw in the towel when this symbol appears. It is a blessed sight indeed, for hope is never truly lost and this symbol alludes to that.

A candle will also appear to represent a person who helps others. The sitter may be a candle unto others, a respite from the storm. Look to other symbols to see if that holds true for the sitter's personality. It might also be that there is a special person in the sitter's life that acts as a guiding light for her, that one person on which she can always depend. If a letter appears with this symbol, it usually refers to that significant other.

CANNABIS LEAF

Natural medicine, earth healing

The United States has come a long way in terms of how it approaches the subject of cannabis. Once universally seen as a scary "gateway drug," cannabis is now viewed by most people as a benign substance that at most makes its users loopy and relaxed. When spotting this symbol in the leaves, it is a sign that the sitter should try a little natural medicine. That *does not* mean that the sitter should begin smoking marijuana. This symbol speaks to the sitter giving alternative medicine a chance. This would include acupuncture, diet changes, lifestyle counseling, homeopathy, herbalism, and more. When this symbol appears, Spirit is encouraging the sitter to try a different method for healing. The sitter may or may not be dealing with current health issues, and remember, she should be referred to a medical professional for specifics beyond this cursory explanation.

Alternatively, when this distinct leaf appears in the teacup, the client may be in need of a little grounding or earth healing. Electricity flows through each human body. It is what keeps our hearts beating. Walking outside, preferably barefoot, can restore the natural ions the human body needs to regulate itself. Also, walks in nature even with shoes on can help, as can hugging trees (trust me, it works) and spending time with animals. All of these activities can lead to a restoration of health through natural means.

CAR

Approaching wealth/financial gain, trip

Here it comes, that fast-approaching automobile, burning rubber and shifting gears. Seeing a distinct image of a car in the tea leaves is a great sign for incoming wealth. Dividends will be paid out, an investment will return big, or that bonus from work will turn out to be fairly substantial. This symbol is not about simply more money coming in, but something that has the potential to build wealth. That can be a lucky windfall, such as lottery or gambling winnings, but usually there has been thought and work behind it. The car does not necessarily represent getting a new car, but it is a possibility as well. More likely, the car foretells money rolling in soon.

Alternatively, a car in the teacup could represent a little road tripping for the client. Sometimes the best solution for your troubles is a little getaway. Maybe the beach or mountains are calling, and this symbol shows up to encourage the client to plan a little trip.

CASTLE

High stature/fame, inheritance, good reputation

When I was a little girl, I imagined myself living in a grand castle off the coast of Ireland or Scotland. I would pretend my room was at the top of the foremost tower. Gazing out of my window, I surveyed all the land before me. I felt like the queen of the world.

Castles are a timeless emblem of stature, rank, and class. So, when this symbol appears in the leaves, it is fortuitous. Perhaps the sitter dreams of a Hollywood career or TikTok fame. Seeing the castle in the cup may mean it can become actual reality. Maybe the sitter is running for office and wants to get a sneak peek at the results. If there are a few more favorable symbols, such as a crown (page 60) or goat (page 73) alongside it, it is almost certainly a slam dunk.

Sometimes a castle can represent an inheritance. This may be known to the sitter, or it can come as a surprise, when she is not aware someone in her life has a little nest egg to leave her. In some instances, this appears to allay a sitter's fears of not receiving a promised inheritance. If scales (page 108) also accompany the castle, this can indicate a legal determination in the sitter's favor in which monies owed will be restored.

In a similar vein as stature or fame, a castle in the leaves can simply stand for a good reputation. This may come after a messy divorce or breakup in which the client's name has been dragged through the mud or sullied by idle gossip. Seeing a castle in the cup makes clients aware that their dignity will return; their minds can ease on this concern.

CAT

Independence, good luck

Ever heard the phrase "herding cats"? You know what makes wrangling cats so hard? They make up their own minds and do not care what you think. They cannot be led, even when treats are involved. When a cat appears in the cup, it may speak to the sitter's personality. This can signal a time of independence for the sitter as she moves out on her own or moves to an entirely new city, potentially starting a new job. Possibly, there is simply too much going on at work, pushing the sitter to quit and go it alone. Maybe a new business idea has been permeating within the sitter's mind and this would be a good time to act on it.

Also, when found in the tea leaves, a cat represents good luck. Sometimes animal guides come to us at certain moments in our lives for specific purposes. To strengthen this bond and to bring in more good fortune for the client, I suggest picking up a cat figurine. It acts as a good luck charm.

CHAIN

Marriage/serious commitment, trouble (if broken), contract

We have all heard the not-so-endearing referral to a spouse as the old ball and chain, haven't we? It is not a pleasant way to describe someone's partner, but it can be a useful memory jogger for this symbol. A chain symbolizes a serious commitment or marriage. The LAWS (page 19) are helpful in this instance, as the appearance changes the symbol's meaning drastically. If the chain is intact, there is a strong bond, a loving marriage, or a committed partnership being referenced. However, if the chain appears broken, there is undoubtedly trouble in paradise. Delve deeper into the cup to sort out which way the relationship is leaning.

If the sitter is not in a romantic relationship or the reading is geared toward business or career questions, a chain can also refer to a contract. This would be a positive sign in terms of closing on a house, landing a job, or growing a business. A contract in its own way also represents a serious commitment. So, in this case, the chain stands for a promise kept.

TIP Remember that your words carry weight. Nothing is more precious to any of us than our personal relationships. So, tread carefully when delivering what can be seen as bad news. In the instance of a broken chain, a relationship may not be doing well. The sitter probably already knows this, unless deeply in denial; however, it can be jarring when a complete stranger points it out. Again, whether reading tea leaves for fun or professionally, be mindful that what is said during any reading has an impact on sitters.

CHAIR

Addition to family, trust, affluence, success

The head of the table normally carries the most importance, necessitating a special chair. What is a king or queen without their throne? If there is a new addition to the family, guess what? There is a need for another chair. So it is when the chair appears in the cup. The sitter may be expecting a new bundle of joy, especially if it is joined by a basket (page 37). There may also be an adoption that comes through. A family addition can also come in the form of extended family, such as when someone gets married.

The client could be looking at taking a new position at work, which will be one of influence and trust, complete with more money. So, if the client has asked about an upcoming promotion, this symbol would mean a resounding yes!

A chair within the cup also means success. Move to this meaning if the sitter denies a new baby, wedding, or promotion is a possibility. This is still a positive omen and portends victory in some area of the sitter's life. The adjacent symbols can help tease out what the success is in reference to.

CHICKEN

Fond childhood memories, spending time with family or old friends

A chicken in every pot! It is an old campaign slogan from the late 1920s, and it evokes warmth and security. So, too, does seeing a chicken in a teacup. Yes, it actually fits! Since a great home-cooked meal elicits warm and tingly feelings, this symbol indicates reminiscing over childhood memories and/or spending time with family and old friends. What is better than gathering with those who know you best, when old inside jokes are shared? Belly laughs that leave your stomach sore for days afterward. Tears shed over tender memories and thoughts of days gone by. In short, the good ole days taste just like chicken! All kidding aside, this can indicate a reconnection with the sitter's past, possibly with a healing taking place. When seen along with a bridge (page 45) or table (page 117), a family reunion is likely or old family rifts will finally be repaired.

Sometimes symbols are literal. With a chicken, this could also represent a pet from childhood, as odd as that might sound. Many farm children have called a trusty chicken their pet. It could also indicate the client grew up on a farm surrounded by chickens. In any case, the client most likely had a pleasant childhood and remembers the past fondly.

CHURCH, MOSQUE, AND/OR TEMPLE

Funeral/wedding/birth, formality/ceremonial, small legacy

A church is a destination for some of the happiest moments in life as well as some of the saddest. From weddings to christenings to deaths, a church is a venue for myriad life events. When it appears in the teacup, it signals that one of these occasions will be upcoming for the sitter. If there is a ring (page 106) or hearts (page 78) accompanying it, a wedding will take place soon. A basket (page 37) and a church represent a baby on the way.

A religious building is also a place where a lot of formality and ceremony take place. Perhaps the sitter is about to graduate, which usually involves a lot of pomp and circumstance. It is also possible that the sitter will undergo a swearing-in ceremony. For example, when someone becomes an attorney or a member of the military, there is a special ceremony for the proceedings.

Depending on the nearby symbols, a small inheritance could also be in the future for the client. Find a castle (page 51), triangle (page 119), or wagon (page 122), and the client stands to receive a legacy from familial connections.

TIP There is no need to tie this symbol to any one specific religion. A mosque or temple can be used interchangeably with a church, as they host the same life events and therefore represent the same meanings.

CIRCLE

Positive sign, good fortune, money, gift

All-encompassing and enclosed, a circle represents the beginning, middle, and end all at once. It is a universal, timeless emblem of completion and success. In the tea leaves, this is a positive sign indeed. In fact, when a circle surrounds another symbol, it strengthens that symbol's meaning as well.

Good fortune is foretold by the circle. Again, apply all the LAWS (page 19) to this symbol for more details. Generally speaking, bigger is better in the case of a circle, and the nearer to the top of the cup the sooner the sitter will enjoy it. This can come in any form that helps elevate the sitter's station in life. Due to its resemblance to coins, circles often refer to being financially fortunate. Remember, financial fortune does not necessarily mean money. It can come in other forms as well, such as job promotions, new cars, or new homes.

The client may also be receiving gifts or money when a circle appears. This omen usually shows up right before a wedding, birthday, or anniversary. Sometimes the gifts will come as a surprise to the client. In terms of additional money, this can come through channels other than work, such as raffle winnings, lottery, tax refunds, or unexpected owed money. Who knows, maybe a friend of the client who loaned her a couple hundred bucks twenty years ago will finally pay it back—stranger things have been foretold in the leaves.

CLOVER

Luck, happiness, prosperity

Clovers, particularly those with four leaves, have always been considered lucky due to their rarity. Some Celtic groups even believed a four-leaf clover would not only grant good luck but also attract fairies. Now, whether enticing fairies brings good or bad luck is another book in itself. But I digress. As for the clover, there has always been a mystique surrounding this deeply green plant.

As already mentioned, this is a sign of luck when found in the teacup, regardless if it has three or four leaves. This symbol does not carry a downside. Every meaning is uplifting and positive. When that is the case, it is a lot easier to help decipher the reading as well.

Beyond luck, happiness and prosperity may also be on the horizon for the sitter. Whatever the sitter may be embarking upon is sure to be met with success, as there will be extra luck available. Find a butterfly (page 47) or a cat (page 52) in the cup as well and there will be a long streak of luck in store.

CROSS

A crucifix is positive for success/happiness
and an X is a warning, inspiration

This symbol is a great example of my mantra, *What I see is meant for me*. Because you use the teacup's handle as a starting point and the cup is turned in a clockwise fashion, this causes the symbols to appear differently oriented within the cup. The key is to go with the image as it first appears to you. If it looks like a cross at first glance, that is usually the correct interpretation. While time should be taken to get the full picture, lingering too long on any one symbol can begin to cast doubt in a reader's mind and the reading can suffer for it.

If the symbol appears as a cross or plus sign, this is a positive omen for incoming success and happiness. However, if the symbol presents more as an X, then a word of caution should be conveyed to the sitter. Spirit is issuing a warning. Check the neighboring symbols to ascertain why the warning is needed.

This symbol can also represent inspiration. It may take the form of an idea that will soon strike the client, causing a breakthrough in an otherwise stagnant situation. The symbol itself may simply be an inspiration to the client to maintain hope while going through a tough time, especially if the client is a person of faith.

TIP Personal bias and baggage have to be addressed within a reader. For example, this symbol comes with religious overtones and possibly strong personal feelings. There needs to be a certain level of objectivity in doing a tea leaf reading. As the reader, you act as a channel, a medium, an outlet that completes the circuit between Spirit and the sitter. Simply let the information flow through you, free of personal opinions regarding certain symbols or life events.

CROWN

Honor, success

What king or queen is complete without a crown? It conveys distinction and honor on whoever wears it. This is also true when a crown appears in the tea leaves. The sitter is sure to receive an honor. This may be from a promotion at work or a special dispensation. It could be a medal or some other distinction, especially if the sitter is military or works as a first responder. Perhaps the sitter is about to earn a degree or certification. As always, the remaining symbols will fill in the blanks.

The crown also represents success. Think of the Triple Crown in horse racing. To win all three of the most prestigious events in the sport is a rare feat. So, the crown in the tea leaves foretells quite the success for the client. Now would be the time to launch a business or social media presence. Moving to the top of a chosen field or profession is likely with this omen. If the crown is the most dominant symbol in the cup, the client would be entering a period of true accomplishment. I always kid my sitters when seeing an emblem such as this to remember the little people like me when they make it big.

DEER

Shy person, good news from a distance

Deer are beautiful, graceful creatures. Very skittish, they are hard to approach in the wild. Much like a rabbit (page 104), a deer within the teacup means that the sitter is a rather shy or introverted person. It may refer to the sitter's baseline personality. Also, it may relate to the sitter's reaction to a current difficult situation in her life. This would be an encouragement to take a more assertive role with this issue.

Conversely, a deer prancing through the teacup is a sign of good news coming, although it might be from a distance. This could mean physically, as in news from a faraway place, or from a source that the client would not naturally expect. If the client is looking for a partner and the deer appears, counsel the client that she may need to put herself out there more in order to entice a lover. This person may not simply fall in her lap. Maybe getting together with friends or a blind date would work better than cruising the dating apps. Again, good news from a distance can come from it, so it is possible that someone from another town may be a great love match.

DOG

Faithful friend, loyalty, help

Has a better friend to humans ever existed? Always loyal, always reliable, always there for cuddles, a doggy in a teacup is lucky. It indicates steadfast and true friends. If there is any doubt regarding the status of a relationship, look to the neighboring symbols. A knife (page 86) or bat (page 38) would indicate false friends. However, hearts (page 78) or circles (page 57) reveal an unbreakable bond, possibly even a friendship that could turn romantic.

But let us go deeper. With tea leaf readings, one must do more than take a cursory glance. Peer into the cup and look more closely. Does the dog seem to be barking? Is it baring its teeth? Is its hair shaggy or short? Each detail adds another layer to the meaning. In the case of snarling teeth, an unknown threat is possible. Some friends may not be as they appear. Location in the cup is also important in determining significance. If the symbol appears near the bottom, it is almost assured that secret enemies are around. However, finding a dog near the rim lets you breathe a sigh of relief, as your friends are most assuredly loyal. As always, take in the full scene in order to get an accurate reading.

With this symbol, the size and stage of development is helpful in deciphering the message. Is the dog full grown or a puppy? If still just a pup, a fresh start or new road is opening up for the sitter. As puppies gleefully live in the moment, this can serve as a reminder not to dwell on the past or take life too seriously. Perhaps the dog is reminiscent of a sitter's past fur baby. Many times, a loved one, even those in animal form, can pop up in our cuppa to say hello. Maybe the sitter has recently gotten a new puppy and is concerned about "replacing" her old friend. Let this be a reassurance that she has her dog's blessing.

Depending on the animal's size, how large an issue the sitter must face and how much it controls her can be determined. Is it tiny like a Chihuahua or overwhelming like a Great Dane? Surrounding symbols can give clues on how to approach and overcome the worries in the sitter's life.

Oftentimes, clients reach out during a low point on their journey. When a pooch appears in the cup, it can be a comfort to the sitter that Spirit knows of her troubles and help is on the way. This is especially true if the dog resembles a golden retriever or Saint Bernard.

TIP Make sure to read the other symbols around even a central symbol in the cup as it all works together to tell a complete story.

DOTS

Emphasize other symbols

With tea leaves, there will be many dots left in the cup after swish-
ing them around. Not every tiny speck of residual leaves needs to
be interpreted, however. In the case of dots, they should be distinct and associated with another symbol in order to be read. This
reduces any confusion related to trying to find meaning where
there isn't any. For example, if there are dots encircling an acorn
(page 30) or car (page 50), cash is on the way because both symbols represent coming riches. In this scenario, the dots increase
the symbols' meanings. Dots are held by the same LAWS as all the
other symbols (page 19). So, pay attention to their appearance. If
the dots are cloudy, it could mean a loss of money for the sitter, as
the murkiness of the symbol can lead to ambiguity in its meaning.
In another example, if there is a bell (page 41) that is surrounded
by dots, then there is sure to be a wedding, one that is probably
taking place pretty soon. Conversely, dots can increase the negativity of a symbol, too. So, if there are many dots around a snake
(page 110) or axe (page 36), the presence of these negative symbols
would carry more weight than normal.

DRAGON

Sudden changes, opportunities after challenges

A fire-breathing dragon is a terrifying mythical creature. Immediately, scenes from *The Hobbit* or *Game of Thrones* come to mind. Known for their love of gold and quick tempers, dragons instill fear and trepidation. As this symbol pertains to the tea leaves, two meanings are revealed. The first is that the sitter will go through unexpected changes. These could be undesirable, such as a job loss or an unplanned move. The changes do not have to be negative, however. There could be a quick turnaround in fortune from an unexpected income source or gift. A legal situation could turn in the sitter's favor. The point is that the changes will come about quickly and usually without much notice, but it does not equate to a "bad" symbol.

Secondly, seeing a dragon can represent an opportunity that shows up after a challenging time. Maybe the client lost a job, only to bounce back with a better position and more pay. Sometimes, an injury can lead to the discovery of a greater health problem. If not for the injury, the more serious underlying condition may have been found too late to treat.

TIP It is good to note that new talents and skills are frequently picked up while dealing with a difficult situation.

ELEPHANT

Strength and wisdom, health and happiness, good luck

Graceful although gigantic, elephants exude strength. Able to squish a human like a bug if they so choose, elephants rarely are aggressive unless provoked. Instead, they are docile creatures who teach and humor humans. When found inside a teacup, this symbol has a few different meanings. As mentioned, elephants are strong. Chances are the sitter is, too, when this symbol appears. The sitter may be the caretaker of the family, or at least the person everyone else goes to with their problems. The sitter has probably gone through trying times where strength and wisdom were the natural by-products.

Beyond an apt description for the client, this omen can also represent health and happiness. If the client enquires about health, this is a positive sign that her health should be improving. Again, always advise the client to follow up with a medical professional.

In feng shui, the Eastern philosophy of arranging décor in living spaces, placing a pair of elephant statues in the entryway of the home is said to bring good luck. The same is true when spotting an elephant in the teacup, although simply seeing one is sufficient for good luck. The elephant joins a list of many symbols such as the clover (page 58), horseshoe (page 80), and cat (page 52) that foretell a sitter's luck improving.

EMOJI

Depending on expression
(i.e., smiley face is good news, frown is sad news, etc.)

With changing times, new symbols should be added to your collection of common tea leaf symbols. In today's society, we express ourselves quite extensively through the use of emojis. The meanings are built in to the images themselves. Seeing a smiley face or frown that looks like a common emoji correlates to its matching emotion. A heart (page 78) already has its own symbology, but it essentially means the same thing as the heart emoji. When seeing a face with tears of joy, the sitter may soon encounter a happy occurrence that is especially meaningful. This could also indicate the sitter is a bit of a jokester and is quite humorous. This is one of those symbols that is truly open to interpretation. It is up to the reader how best to read it. Remember my mantra, *What I see is meant for me.* What appears to the reader first and what connotation that symbol contains is the best method for divining the symbol's meaning. As always, the rest of the cup's symbols will shed additional light.

EYE

Protective symbol, new way of seeing things, careful in dealings

The eyes are said to be windows to the soul. They are essentially two-way mirrors; one side receives the external world while the other projects the inner. This may be why, dating back at least five thousand years, the concept of the evil eye developed. Picture it. Glug, the caveman, is regaling his fellow Paleolithic pals with his latest hunting adventures, bragging yet again about how many mammoths he took down with a single shot. Around the campfire's flickering light, many an eye roll can be seen. Not more than two days later, Glug is found dead from a stampede of mammoths. Bad luck? Or the work of the infamous evil eye?

Many people confuse the nazar (the evil eye pendant) with the evil eye itself, but actually it is what protects against someone throwing evil at you. Much as it is with seeing an eye symbol in your teacup. It is a protective symbol. The sitter can rest easy knowing that although there may be some negativity in her life, she is divinely protected against it. This is a positive omen indeed.

Also, the client may be going through a new phase of life and looking at things differently. Possibly old problems are being seen through a different lens, and the client is open to change.

Due to the connection with the eye and possible negativity toward the client, this symbol can also be a warning that some untrustworthy people could try to take advantage of the client. The client should be careful in any possible dealings during this time. In this situation, I tend to counsel the client to trust her gut and instincts.

FEATHER

Need to be more serious, news coming

Fluttering on the breeze like a feather may sound like a dream, seemingly without a care in the world, but sometimes we have to come back down to earth. This symbol within the teacup is a reminder of just that. There may be a need for the sitter to face something head on and to be more serious about the situation at hand. This usually shows up for a younger sitter who has been postponing a major life decision, such as finding that first grown-up job. I have seen this symbol pop up around pivotal birthdays, such as the Big 3-0, when life normally turns a bit more serious for us all.

Alternatively, seeing a feather means news is coming to the client. This is an excellent symbol to apply all the LAWS (page 19), as the meaning can change significantly without them. If the feather is distinct, the news will be good. However, a cloudy or misshapen feather can foretell bad news. If there are additional symbols representing news, like an angel (page 34), arrow (page 35), or horse (page 79), these can aid in figuring out if the feather signifies good or bad news as well.

FISH

Wisdom, good news from afar, Pisces

A fishy friend swimming around in the tea leaves is always a welcome sight. It is a good omen, no matter how it is interpreted. To begin with, a fish represents wisdom. It may refer to the sitter's own innate perception. Sometimes sitters come to a reader in moments of doubt. They face big issues and want to be pointed in the right direction. When this symbol appears, it is Spirit's gentle way of redirecting the sitter back to her own inner guidance system. The fish can also refer to the wisdom that will be gained from the current situation that the sitter is going through. Even when bad things happen in life, often, lessons are learned from them.

The fish symbol may also mean that the client has good news coming from afar. This usually refers to information coming from a distant land, possibly a foreign country, or at least a fair physical distance from the client. Back when tea leaf readings originally started, receiving news from a distant place took a long time to reach the client. However, with the advancement of technology, good news, even from remote places, can be relayed quickly. So, receiving information from a far-off place does not have to mean it will take a long time for the client to receive it. The fish also represents the zodiac sign of Pisces, which might be in reference to the sitter's own sign or someone who plays a significant role in her life. See the zodiac entry for Pisces (page 131) for more details.

FLOWERS

Good fortune, happy marriage

Who doesn't love a beautiful bouquet of flowers? The aroma, colors, and vibe they bring to a room are unmatched. They have the power to brighten anyone's day. In much the same vein, finding flowers in the teacup will improve the sitter's day. Flowers represent good fortune. Paired with either a circle (page 57) or triangle (page 119), double the prosperity is likely. This is an excellent omen to receive when the sitter is prepping for a job interview or getting ready to launch an online business. It indicates that these endeavors will turn out to be fruitful.

Flowers, frequently sent as a gift in relationships, also represent a happy marriage. If the client is already married, the relationship is a healthy and stable one. If the client is engaged, her mind can rest easy that her marriage will be one filled with love and joy. Specific flowers can denote more specific meanings. For example, a rose signifies love, a daisy for friendship, and a grouping of flowers simply strengthens the upcoming good fortune.

FROG

Pride will not carry you far, look within

Frogs are amphibians who transform from tadpoles to adults within their lifespan. Naturally slimy creatures, they have been portrayed in fairy tales as poor substitutes for princes. As for frog symbology within the tea leaves, this symbol requires a delicate delivery. First off, always apply the LAWS (page 19) to each symbol. Once the location, appearance, way, and size have been accounted for, the reason for the frog in the cup will be much clearer. As always, the surrounding symbols offer clues as to why the sitter may need to receive this particular message.

The first interpretation of a frog is that the sitter has been rather boastful or perhaps not 100 percent honest about life achievements or events. This is a kind of fake-it-until-you-make-it personality trait. Individuals like this may be clever and often charm their way into situations. However, when the rubber meets the road, they cannot back up all their claims. Again, there are no judgments to be made here. Simply stated, the frog represents a warning that unchecked pride usually does go before a fall. Positive self-esteem and self-love are always a must, but if the ego is overly inflated and leading the sitter astray, that should be mentioned.

So, for most tea leaf readings, when the frog appears, it is an opportunity for the sitter to look within. Sitters may come with several problems stacked up and be completely dumbfounded at how they have arrived at such a point in their lives. Upon further reflection, it soon becomes clear that it is time to take some personal responsibility. In a reading such as this, the sitter very well may have an epiphany of sorts that, once some inner work is accomplished, more positive life events will occur.

GOAT

Success in any venture, obstinate, Capricorn

A goat found in a tea leaf reading means success in any form for the client. This is most likely due to the client's strong nature. This type of success comes about from hard work and a can-do attitude. Whether it be in business, relationships, or health, the outcome will be a positive one.

A goat also represents the zodiac sign of Capricorn. People born under this sign are strong-willed, tenacious, and almost always successful in whatever endeavors they pursue. When found in the teacup, the symbol of the goat means the same. The sitter may be a Capricorn sun sign or have a lot of Capricorn placements in her chart. If the sitter was born under another sign, then she has many of Capricorn's attributes. This can indicate the sitter is headstrong and persistent.

While goats and their zodiac counterparts alike can be determined, that level of intensity can sometimes turn into obstinacy. Spirit may be alluding to the sitter being a little too stubborn over an issue or that she is dealing with someone else who is unwilling to compromise. Look to the surrounding symbols to clear up any confusion.

GUN

Discord, be careful

A gun in most contexts is not something anyone is excited to see. It usually means the situation is dicey and there is a fear that things could get violent. When seen in the tea leaves, a gun represents discord. There is probably much chaos surrounding the sitter at this time. Relationships may be suffering from fights and miscommunications. Work might feel like a daily obstacle course the sitter has to endure. Any way you spin it, this is not an uplifting omen. Thankfully, within a tea leaf reading, the message never comes down to a single symbol. Although the firearm represents discord, the neighboring symbols may show the solution to the sitter's troubles.

Also, following the LAWS (page 19) will give more details on this subject. If the gun is pointing toward the handle, this is trouble coming at the sitter. However, when it points away, the sitter could be causing some of this trouble with her own actions. Be delicate with the delivery of this symbol's message.

When the gun appears in the tea leaves, advise the client to be cautious. There is disharmony in the air, and a thoughtful approach would be best. Surrounding symbols will offer further details to which particular area of life this may be in reference to.

TIP In general, when there is strife or struggle present, being vigilant is the best course of action.

HAMMER

Triumph over difficulties, persistence, driving a point home

A hammer is a tool used to build new things and fix those in need of repair. Either way, the result of a hammer's hard work is an achievement. In much the same way, a hammer found in the teacup indicates a triumph over difficulties for the sitter. This is a welcomed sight to the sitter when experiencing hard times. This conveys that there is light at the end of the proverbial tunnel.

The hammer also represents persistence. And with this symbol, that persistence is paying off. The client has waged battle but kept going in the face of adversity. This leads to victory over the client's worries. If a hammer is found alongside a goat (page 73), the client is definitely a persistent individual, which is an admirable trait.

This symbol also alludes to making one's point a little too much. Perhaps the sitter is worried about a situation and has been making that known to her significant other over and over and over again. Maybe the sitter wanted to make someone aware of an issue and belabored the point past its usefulness. After looking to neighboring symbols for more context, it may be best to tactfully advise the sitter that her point has been made, and it is more than okay to let the matter play itself out from this point forward.

HAND

Friendly, warning, friendship extended, loss of opportunity

Hands are a means through which different emotions can be conveyed. A thumbs-up indicates a good job, and holding up the index finger means "we're number one" all over the world. An extension of the middle finger may indicate a slight difference in opinion over one's driving skills. All in all, a hand can tell quite the story without ever speaking a word.

Within the tea leaves, a hand speaks volumes. Let's look at the LAWS (page 19) in action when defining this symbol. If the hand is clearly defined within the tea leaves, this indicates friendliness. The sitter is most likely a true and loyal person and can be counted on as a trustworthy friend. However, if the symbol is unclear or cloudy, then the hand serves as a warning. It acts almost like Stop, Halt, No Outlet, and Do Not Travel This Way signs. When added to the other symbols in the cup, the reader should get a sense of what the sitter is being warned about. If the hand is facing the handle, a friendship will be extended to the sitter. Conversely, if the hand is facing away, there could be a loss of an opportunity for the sitter.

HAT

New occupation/job offer, success in life

A person who wears many hats is a person who has many responsibilities. So, when a hat appears in the tea leaves, a new job or entirely new occupation for the client is possible. Also, if the client questions whether to take a job, the answer is yes. Many times, clients have already made their decisions, but it is always nice to receive confirmation. As we all do, they want to know if they are making the "right" decision.

The hat also represents attaining success. A top hat is synonymous with wealth and success. A tip of the hat also shows respect. So, in a sense, this is Spirit's way of tipping the hat to the sitter and saying, "job well done."

TIP The hat symbol allows readers to flex those psychic skills because sitters are often flabbergasted by a fact simply being stated. Confidence is key to any good reading. Self-doubt likes to creep in and cause you to frame all the information you're reading as a question. Are you looking for a new job? Could it be possible you want to change careers? Instead, it is much more powerful to declare, "I see you are going to be changing careers or at least get a new job."

HEART

Love, marriage, good things to come

A universal symbol for love, the heart is an overwhelmingly positive symbol. If the sitter wants to know if she will find love, this is a yes. If the sitter wants to know if her current relationship is based on true feelings, this is also a yes. When there are two hearts touching, it is a great match. If the heart appears broken, the sitter may soon go through a breakup, but the remaining symbols in the cup will help determine that. When paired with certain symbols, such as a sword (page 116), a heart may indicate that the sitter's heart has been damaged by previous relationships and now she finds herself in the right one.

This symbol also indicates marriage. If there is a ring (page 106) in conjunction with the heart, a proposal is imminent. By using all the LAWS (page 19), you can determine when the client may receive the big question. Of course, the client may not want to know the exact details, since being surprised for this life event is fun and romantic.

When the client is not involved in a romantic relationship, the symbol's meaning becomes a herald of good things to come. A heart in the cup is a beacon of hope. Although the client's current situation may not be ideal, this omen comes to offer a light at the end of the tunnel. This heart can also represent the love of Spirit, reaching out to the client.

HORSE

Close friendship, lover coming, good news, journey

The Romany people's relationship with horses is long and deeply personal. They pulled our *vardos* (wagons); they brought beauty into our lives; they became our friends; and that is what seeing a horse in the tea leaves means—a truly close bond. Sometimes sitters question the strength of their relationships. They want to know if someone is loyal or not. When this symbol appears, the sitter's worries can be allayed, as a horse speaks to a secure relationship.

A horse also represents a new love entering the sitter's life. In romance novels, a lover almost always shows up atop a noble steed. So, it stands to reason a horse in the tea leaves would indicate the potential for romance as well.

If the horse appears to be running, it becomes a sign of good news is on its way to the client—since horses have long been used to help transport messages (think the Pony Express). Similarly, because horses have been used as a method of transportation for many years, seeing a horse in the tea leaves can also signal an upcoming journey. Look to the surrounding symbols to determine when it may be taking place and to where.

HORSESHOE

Good luck, success in choosing a partner

Romany people put great store in the luck of a horseshoe. Hung over a doorway, a horseshoe is said to catch all good luck (*baxt*). So, when spotting a horseshoe in the cup, count the sitter lucky. When combined with a clover (page 58) or butterfly (page 47), the luck will overflow. If the sitter mentions buying a scratch-off ticket or traveling to Vegas, the chances are favorable the sitter could come home a winner. This may also mean it's a good time to start a new project or something that the sitter has been afraid to do up until this point. A little luck helps a person get over the initial nerves of heading down a new path.

A horseshoe is also favorable for a client interested in finding a partner, whether business or romantic. For example, maybe the client has an idea, but does not have the capital to get the business off the ground. In this case, the symbol might mean that the perfect person to help fund the sitter's dream will come along. In terms of romance, this is a good sign that the client will not be single for much longer, which alerts the client that she is on the right path and the perfect partner is on the way.

HOURGLASS

Urgency, act quickly, imminent danger

This omen has an intense energy attached to it. An hourglass, a timekeeping device dating back to the eighth century BCE, marks the passage of time with sand falling from one glass bulb to another. When seeing this in the tea leaves, imagine the sand is just about to run out. Time is short, and this urgency needs to be conveyed to the sitter. Make sure not to alarm your sitter when passing along this message.

The meaning is simple: The time to act is now. Perhaps the client has been dragging her feet on making an important decision. Counsel the client that life cannot move forward until action is taken. Sometimes worrying about how something will turn out paralyzes a person's ability to grow. This is a nudge from the Universe to tell the client there is no time like the present. Get a move on!

Due to hesitancy, the sitter may have pushed the boundaries of time here. This does not necessarily mean there is a tragedy or catastrophe looming, but there may be a real danger of the sitter missing out on an opportunity she will regret losing. Again, take this symbol into account along with all the others in the cup, and the message will clear up.

TIP Let this symbol be a reminder to choose your words carefully, and make sure to have that full picture in view before giving the reading. The hourglass doesn't necessarily have to take on a negative feel. It is simply a wake-up call sounding, not a death knell.

HOUSE

Contented life, business success

When this symbol appears in the tea leaves, things are good in the sitter's home. The sitter has reached a level of satisfaction that is fulfilling and peaceful. This means there is order within the home. It can mean literally within the sitter's house itself, but usually it is more metaphorical in its meaning. Normally, the sitter has attained a sense of ease and contentment with all domestic issues. Her relationship is good, and the work-life balance is good. The person may have come for a general reading and be open to whatever message Spirit brings instead of looking for a solution to some problem. What a lovely reading to give!

This is also a great sign of business success, and it is excellent for investments or the purchase of real estate for expanding a business. When work or business is going well, most other things in life go well, too. If a house appears with a hat (page 77) or anchor (page 33), do not hesitate to let the client know that any business-related issues will turn out wonderfully.

INFINITY SYMBOL

Limitless, boundless

The infinity symbol looks like a lazy eight, lying on its side rather than sitting upright like the number. The orientation of this symbol is important when determining its meaning. If it is sitting upright and looks like the number eight, check the meaning under the entry for numbers (page 99). If it appears as the infinity symbol (lying on its side), interpret it as follows.

The infinity symbol represents the limitless and boundless potential of the sitter. This symbol is sent to remind the sitter that she is more than just a human being. She is directly connected to the Source of all that is. Counsel the client that she is capable of achieving whatever she puts her mind to, and this is an endorsement from Spirit of just that. This means that the sitter should not be putting any limits on what she thinks she is capable of achieving.

Also, this is a great symbol to receive if the sitter is hoping her manifestations (page 25) will come true. There is a certain amount of faith that is involved in manifesting. So, this symbol appears when the sitter may be in need of a little more hope in her life.

KEY

Problems solved, unlock new opportunities

When you see a key in the cup, there is true cause for hope. Like a key opening a closed door, a key in the cup can signal to the sitter that she has the key to solving her problems. A new insight or different way to think about the problem may be all that is needed to fix the issues at hand. The solution may come from someone else entirely, but it is coming nonetheless. Also, a key represents unlocking new opportunities for the client. A new option with work or romance may be found, and this key can unlock the way forward.

TIP Let's face it: Rarely do clients come for readings because life is great and they simply want confirmation. More often, sitters come because they need help with issues. There are bills piling up, work is causing a headache, or there is trouble in relationships. They want reassurance that everything will be okay. Therefore, never give false hope. That is not the job of the reader. The reader's role is simply to convey the message given within the cup.

KITE

Reaching great heights, extended voyage, restless at the moment

When a kite is seen in the teacup, it represents reaching great heights, much like a kite itself. This symbol indicates that the sitter is on track to do big things. If the sitter is at the beginning of any venture and inquires as to how it will turn out, the answer is "pretty well." This omen foretells great success, and this symbol can even allude to stardom for the sitter. Whenever a kite appears, I take the opportunity to encourage the sitter to try some manifesting (page 25). It is an excellent indication that the timing is right for the sitter to reach for the stars. Advise the sitter to write down what she would most like to see come to pass in her life and then to send that energy out into the Universe. She may be surprised to find her manifestations come to fruition quickly when the kite is present.

Since a kite can travel pretty far into the sky, it can also represent an extended voyage. The client may have a vacation planned that will end up lasting longer than expected, or perhaps a business trip will turn into a short-term stay.

Due to the energy associated with the kite, the client may find herself feeling impatient. Many times, clients feel that changes are about to come, but they are not exactly sure when or what they may be and therefore have a tendency to become a little anxious, waiting for something to happen. Instruct the client that she is simply picking up on the shifting energies in her life, which is a good thing.

KNIFE

Warning of trouble, false friends, broken relationship

Although a knife is not the most uplifting symbol, each one plays its part when reading tea leaves. A knife warns of trouble, and it is not happy news to deliver. The type of trouble the sitter may be facing will become clear once you take into account any surrounding symbols, such as a hat (page 77) or chain (page 53). For example, the knife paired with a hat means that the trouble could be found at work with a possible job loss. When the knife is coupled with a chain, this trouble might result in marital woes.

When you see a knife, look at its relationship to the cup's handle. Is the blade facing it? This means that someone might have the upper hand in a situation with the sitter. Conversely, if the blade is facing away from the handle, then some treachery may be afoot, but the sitter will come out on top.

A knife can also be a warning of fake friends. If a knife appears alongside a bat (page 38), then the sitter is sadly surrounded by some phony people. Sometimes when a knife appears, the sitter knows right away who it is in reference to. But there are times when the sitter is clueless. Keep a lookout for letters or numbers with the knife, as those can give clues as to who this mystery troublemaker is.

Also, a knife is a sign that the client's relationships may be a little rocky during this period. In fact, they are probably more than a little rocky; they are probably outright broken. Again, the client probably has an inkling of this situation, but if she appears unaware, it is the reader's job to put the puzzle pieces together.

LADDER

Travel after great success, opportunities for advancement,
keep going/moving

Ever play Chutes and Ladders as a kid? The chutes tossed you down a few pegs, while the ladders always helped you race ahead. Ladders in the tea leaves are also awesome signs.

The first meaning is that after a great success, the sitter may be up for some travel. How could this scenario play out? Perhaps there has been a recent graduation, and afterward the sitter plans a vacation to celebrate. It may indicate a honeymoon after a successful wedding. Time to hit up New Orleans to celebrate an accomplishment Big Easy style. It is always best to give the sitter a real-life situation instead of simply mechanically repeating, "Oh. I see you'll travel after a great success." The tea leaves may give you the exact details, but if not, a general example still helps to make it real for the sitter.

Seeing a ladder in relation to work is a positive sign, since everyone is familiar with moving up the ladder. Within the context of work, it means you are gaining responsibility and stature. The sitter may be soon moving and shaking within her career.

A ladder is also a sign that someone is moving, so check any surrounding symbols. If there is a boat (page 44), then there will be a physical change of residence and it will be beneficial to the client. It can also mean there are opportunities being presented to the client to advance in life and now is the time to seize them.

LAMP

Illumination, secrets revealed, postponement,
lost property recovered

A lamp brings light to the darkness and helps expose what was once hidden. By the same token, when a lamp appears in the tea leaves, insights are made. This symbol can refer to the fact that the sitter is going through a period of awakening. The world has officially entered the Age of Aquarius, a time foretold as the moment humanity collectively becomes more conscious. So, it is not unusual to have a client undergoing a period of revelation. Subjects that were once taboo have become more acceptable to study, and this symbol tends to pop up for sitters who are curious about the occult and other mysterious studies.

Beyond the ancient mysteries of the Universe, more mundane secrets may also be discovered by the client. This symbol indicates a moment of clarity will be reached by the client. Betrayals and heartaches can be imminent with this symbol, but make sure to check the remaining symbols in the cup to be certain. This is another symbol in which the importance of following the LAWS (page 19) is so important. If the lamp appears in the bottom of the cup, a postponement of some type is likely. As it is easier to find something when the light is on, when a lamp appears in the tea-cup, there is a great probability of locating a lost object if the sitter has lost anything recently and hopes to get it back.

TIP Tea leaf symbols share a similarity with real estate, as they are both all about location, location, location.

LEAF

New page/chapter/time of life, messages/letters

"Turning over a new leaf" is a common phrase that refers to making positive behavior changes in one's life, starting again, and bringing in fresh energy. When seeing a leaf shape, and not the actual tea leaves themselves, the sitter may be at a point in life to make some changes. The sitter may have some old habits she would like to kick or want to pick up some healthy ones. Opportunities should be opening up for the sitter, which will produce major changes. This symbol tends to arrive before a major life transition, such as heading off to college, moving to a new city, sobriety, weddings, deaths, births, or any of those pivotal moments that cause the sitter's book of life to turn the page.

It is also possible that the client may be receiving a message that helps her move into this new phase. There could news that she has been accepted into her first-pick college or grad school. A legal determination for a client who is awaiting a disability claim to be approved might be en route. These types of messages can change anyone's life. It is also possible that a new job opening or house, which the client thought was unachievable, may suddenly become available and change everything.

LETTERS
(ALPHABETICAL)

Names, places

Whenever there is an alphabetical letter formed in the tea leaves, it is to be taken literally. It can represent the first initial of the sitter's name or someone else in the sitter's life. It is rare that there will be enough letters to spell an entire word. However, if that happens, it is important to take note of that word. When a letter appears, it can also represent the name of the sitter's future romantic partner. It could even stand for the name of the sitter's boss or good friend. Ultimately, no symbol shows up by chance. So, pay particular attention to letters as they leave little room for interpretation and have a more straightforward impact on the reading.

Depending on the other symbols, a letter can refer to a location as well. Perhaps the tea leaves show a move in the client's future and the letter will point to where it will be. If the tea leaf reading is being done for mediumship, this letter can refer to a passed loved one's name. It can also give clues to a guide's name.

LINES

Journey, direction/progress, movement

When there are clear lines in the teacup, it can signify a journey for the sitter. This can be literal or metaphorical. Perhaps the sitter is about to set sail for distant shores. Maybe the sitter is setting off on a journey of the soul. Applying the LAWS (page 19) is useful when dealing with lines in the cup. If the leaves form distinct lines, this is a sign of a trip being undertaken. If the lines are wavy or broken, there could be a delay, but it will still take place. For example, that might mean a concert will get cancelled but later rescheduled. Or a cruise may get postponed but not indefinitely. How long or short are the lines? Based on the length, it can be determined if this will be a short or long trip.

Lines can also indicate progress or direction in the client's life. If the lines track back toward the handle, there is forward momentum. However, if the lines are on the opposite side of the cup away from the handle, the client may feel like life is going backward. Additional symbols will bring more details to light.

Lines also show movement on a project or situation in the sitter's life. Pay attention to the direction in which they fall. Are they near the handle or the rim? This means the movement will take place soon, most likely within days to a couple of weeks. If nearer the bottom or away from the handle, then things may take a little more time before moving ahead.

LION

Powerful friend, position will improve, leadership recognized, Leo

Lions are said to be the kings of the jungle. No one questions their authority in the animal kingdom. Their roar alone has been known to instill fear in the bravest of hearts. So, when a lion appears in the cup, *powerful* should be the first word associated with this symbol. In fact, if this symbol shows up, the sitter must have a pretty influential friend who holds some type of political clout or a certain level of fame and will be beneficial to the sitter. Through this friendship, new doors may open for the client.

When this animal appears in a tea leaf reading, there is a good chance the sitter's station in life is soon to improve. In general, when this symbol appears, the sitter's life is on the upswing.

As the lion rules over the jungle, the client's leadership skills may come to the forefront. This could result in a promotion at work. Look for a ladder (page 87) in the tea leaves to strengthen this meaning.

The lion is also the symbol for the zodiac sign of Leo. The client may have been born under this sign or carries many of its attributes, such as generosity and leadership. When I encounter this symbol, I always encourage the client to be proud of her inner strength and to not hold back in pursuing her passions.

MAN

Visitor

Seeing a man in the cup means company will soon come calling, which may or may not be expected by the client. Although the figure may appear male, the symbol does not necessarily mean the visitor will be male. With a simple symbol such as this, the LAWS (page 19) lend much more detail. Where is the man located within the cup? Is the image distinct or cloudy? Which way is the man facing within the cup? How big is the symbol in relation to the surrounding symbols?

For example, imagine a clearly defined man facing the handle of the cup near the rim. The man is much bigger than the rest of the symbols within the reading. Due to the symbol's location within the cup, this visit will happen soon. The well-outlined appearance indicates this will be someone that will positively impact the sitter's life. Since the man is facing the handle, this visit is most likely going to be a surprise for the sitter, as she is not in control of the visit. The relatively large size of the symbol indicates that this visit will ultimately have a big influence on the sitter's life. If I saw this symbol along with an acorn (page 30) and car (page 50), I would advise the sitter that this visitor may bring about a big financial upswing in her life.

MERMAID

Creative phase, possible trip, melding of two worlds

Mermaids have long been held as mythical creatures, luring sailors to their deaths. Maybe not the most positive light to be painted in, but it does require a certain amount of creativity to trick human beings. Similarly, the meaning in tea leaf readings is that the sitter will move into a creative phase of life. Through harnessing these creative skills, the sitter can go to the next level in life.

Alternatively, a possible journey could be coming up for the client, one requiring travel over a body of water. Most likely this is a long-distance trip that will be centered either around an ocean, such as a beach trip, or involve crossing an ocean en route.

As mermaids are a mash-up of fish and humans, it is no coincidence that as a symbol in the tea leaves a mermaid indicates the sitter may also be merging two worlds in her personal life. This can happen in the form of blending two families together through either marriage or combining households. Combining two worlds can also take place through integrating work and home life. Perhaps the sitter wants to start a business based on a lifelong hobby. Taking this interest and building it out of her home would be a way to blend those two worlds.

MOON

Innermost feelings, pay attention to dreams/intuition, new undertakings

Ah, the mysterious moon. Every month it goes through a complete transformation from new moon to full. It sets out on a new journey at the start of each cycle and comes full circle. Emergency rooms and jails around the world will testify to a full moon's effect on both patients and inmates. Humans are made up of about 60 percent water, and the moon affects the tides and humans equally. Heightened emotions are a full moon's calling card. So, when the moon appears in the tea leaves, the sitter needs to pay attention to her innermost feelings. What is coming up at this time for the sitter? There could be old patterns or traumas coming to the surface. It is time for the sitter to face these emotions and work through them.

When the moon appears, the client should pay close attention to her dreams. They may prove to be prophetic or offer a key to an issue of concern. Also, the client may find her intuitive insights are off the charts.

New beginnings could also be taking place for the sitter, especially if the moon appears to be a crescent as seen with a new moon. Paired with a hat (page 77), it is sure to be a new job. Seen with a heart (page 78) and it could be the start of a beautiful romance.

MOUNTAINS

Ambition with challenges, achievement through effort, big dreams

Mountain climbers have often been asked why they attempt such incredible feats. Sometimes it is reward enough simply to push one's limits. When a mountain appears in the teacup, it represents the sitter's ambition. However, much like reaching a mountain's peak, challenges will be encountered along the way. With this symbol, acknowledge the sitter's determination, and counsel her that she may need to rely upon it in order to achieve her goals. There will be obstacles, but her tenacity will see her through.

In addition, when a mountain forms in the leaves, it symbolizes that the client will reach a great achievement, but it will require work. As with climbing a mountain, it takes time, effort, practice, and patience.

Mountains also represent that the client has big dreams. These do not constitute average, run-of-the-mill dreams. A mountain indicates this person has huge plans for the future and most likely the accompanying willpower that will help her achieve them all. When a mountain appears along with a kite (page 85), which I have only ever seen a few times, I know my client will truly make her mark on the world.

MOUSE

Thief/burglary possible, neglected opportunities, be cautious

A cute little mouse scurrying away with a piece of cheese always got a laugh in the cartoons, but not so much if it is spotted in a tea leaf reading. This is a clear warning to the sitter.

The first meaning is that either a physical theft of personal property is possible, or given today's technology, the sitter may need to be on guard for identity theft. This can also represent a thief being present in the sitter's life, such as a money manager, friend, or family member that has something to do with the sitter's financial affairs. Again, this symbol alone can be alarming if conveyed to the sitter all by itself. However, if a mouse appears in the cup alongside a heart (page 78), my message to the sitter would change drastically. If the other symbols corroborated it, I would advise the sitter that I see that someone has stolen her heart.

If the other teacup symbols tend to be leaning more negative, the simple advice for the client is to be cautious in all dealings. Maybe update a home or car alarm system and passwords. Double-check all financial matters. There is no need to panic the sitter.

A mouse also speaks to neglected opportunities, which the sitter is stealing from herself. Make sure to remind the sitter that not every possibility stays around forever. This will be doubly clear if you also see an hourglass (page 81). Time is ticking and the sitter needs to get a move on.

MUSHROOM

Rapid growth, advancement through expansion and growth

Ever see a mushroom pop up overnight in the backyard after a good rain? Then, before you know it, there is an entire network of fungi running along the roots of a tree. Mushroom growth is explosive and quick, sometimes giving no outward indication ahead of time. The same goes for seeing a mushroom in a teacup. The nearer to the bottom of the cup, the more rapid the growth will be. This could be in regard to finances, career, or even spiritual endeavors. Investments would be a safe bet when a mushroom appears in a reading. This symbol may also indicate that the sitter's online and social media presence is taking off. Perhaps the sitter is interested in learning about her psychic skills. This omen would be a positive indicator that her spiritual journey may expand quickly.

Similarly, another meaning is that the client will experience advancement through newfound growth and expansion. If the client already has a business, she should consider opening a new location or expanding to online sales, as the mushroom is an excellent sign that the timing is right to do so. Also, the personal growth or expansion the client has recently gone through, or will shortly be going through, can lead to advancement in other areas of her life. For example, she may start a spiritually based business or find a job that offers more fulfillment in alignment with her new sense of self.

NUMBERS

Denotes passage of time and amounts

Like alphabetical letters (page 90), numbers are also to be taken at face value. They signify passages of time: days, weeks, months, or years. These symbols follow the LAWS (page 19). If near the rim, it usually refers to a range of days to a couple of weeks. If found in the middle of the cup, the timing falls into the area of several weeks to months away. At the bottom of the cup, the timing relates to a year out. Numbers can also represent amounts. For example, if a basket (page 37) is in the cup, denoting future pregnancies, and the sitter inquires as to how many children overall she will have, seeing an accompanying number can give that answer.

TIP Angel numbers are popular. They are number sequences that usually contain repetition (1111, 2222, etc.) intended to send a message to a person to help them through a difficult time or as an acknowledgment that the person is on the right path. These are believed to be sent by someone's guardian angels, guides, or God. If one of these numbers comes up in the tea leaves, it is important to take note of it. The rather extensive list of angel numbers exceeds the scope of what can be touched upon in this book, but in this example, I would recommend relying on either your prior knowledge of what the angel number means or doing a quick online check and going with the meaning that intuitively makes the most sense for the reading at hand.

OWL

Wisdom, wise advice, learning

Owls are universally linked with wisdom due to their heightened senses and excellent night vision. In fact, the ancient Greeks found owls' vision so powerful they proposed it was powered by a mystical inner light. They associated owls with Athena, the Goddess of Wisdom. Seeing an owl in the teacup indicates wisdom. If the owl is facing away from the handle, the sitter herself is most likely the wise one in this scenario, as the owl is projecting wisdom onto the situation from the sitter's point of view. Or it is possible the sitter is in need of a little wisdom, which is an indicator that either the client will receive sage advice she should take (possibly during the reading) or could be dispensing it to someone else. Maybe the client is the friend everyone else comes to for advice, and it is becoming a problem for her. Also, it is a possibility the sitter is headed back to school or taking additional certifications/classes for her current line of work. Again, check surrounding symbols to nail it down.

PALM TREE

Retiring well off, success, honor

Palm trees are a known symbol for the good life. Beautiful locales such as California, Florida, and Hawaii are lined with them. They evoke relaxation, peace, and luxury. Tapping into this energy, the symbol represents the same. This symbol represents long-term success for the sitter. In order to retire with a healthy nest egg, the sitter must be successful throughout her life. So, this omen foretells of present and future achievements. A palm tree can also represent somewhere the client may want to live. If there are surrounding symbols representing a move, such as a broom (page 42), then this is a fair assessment to make.

A palm tree showing up in the cup also represents success and honor. When these two are combined, the client may have the potential to work in a prestigious field, such as law or medicine. I have found a palm tree show up quite frequently when the sitter is a part of the military or is a first responder. This usually means the sitter will receive a distinction for going above and beyond in her role.

PIG

Good luck that might incite jealousy, careful of overindulgence

When a piggy pops up in the teacup, it is lucky for the sitter. In many cultures, pigs are seen as good luck charms. In fact, the sitter may want to pick up a pig ornament to strengthen the luck. Although the sitter is in for some good luck, be aware it might come with a side of haters. As one's success often does, it can cause some jealousy among so-called friends. This usually comes with the purchase of new cars and homes. The sitter may get a great new job that causes some friction. It is important to remind a client that what is meant for her will always come to her, and what is meant for others will find them. They are only responsible for their own emotions, not others'.

This symbol can also stand as a warning to be careful of any overindulgences, be it with money, food, alcohol, or drugs. Pigs are known to be excessive and can consume literally anything, including other pigs. Spirit's message to the sitter is that while good luck and success may come more readily, it is wise to exercise some self-control. While it is tempting when the good life sets in, it is best to maintain balance.

QUESTION MARK

Important question, something unknown

When a question mark appears in the tea leaves, an important question may be asked of the sitter. There is also the chance that the sitter needs to ask one of herself. In terms of being asked something, the most likely question would be in reference to getting married. If there are additional symbols that relate to getting engaged, such as a ring (page 106), then this is definitely the subject of the question. With regards to the sitter asking a question, this might be more introspective. The client may take a look at her current situation and ask important questions aimed at inner growth and healing.

Alternatively, this symbol can represent an unknown within the sitter's life. As odd as this may seem for a tea leaf reading, this may need to remain unknown to the sitter at this time. There may be other clues in the leaves as to what this mystery is, but if it remains unclear, simply advise the sitter that Spirit will reveal it in their own time. Sometimes we have to be patient and let things unfold. Even psychics cannot know everything all the time.

RABBIT

Need for bravery, timid, fertility

A rabbit in the cup is a call for the sitter to show some bravery. Maybe the sitter's fears are getting the best of her. There could be a dream that a person wants to pursue, but a constant barrage of what-ifs or overthinking can cause analysis paralysis in which the sitter never gets started. When a rabbit pops up in the teacup, it is okay to let the sitter know that she is braver than she gives herself credit for.

It could be possible that past events or trauma have caused the client to play somewhat timid with life, but with the appearance of the rabbit, Spirit is advising that now is the time for action. The leaves are explaining it is okay to take a chance. It is hard to play while only watching from the sidelines.

Rabbits are famously known for their ability to multiply. So, based on nearby symbols, such as a basket (page 37) or bell (page 41), this may be an omen that a baby is on the way. Apply all the LAWS (page 19) to this symbol, if the sitter is interested to know, and an approximate time and possible gender of the baby could be ascertained from the leaves.

RELIGIOUS FIGURES

(Jesus, Moses, Mother Mary, Buddha, Krishna, etc.),
Ascended masters, spirituality

Jesus and Mother Mary famously seem to appear on the most mundane items, from pieces of toast to cliffs. So, the tea leaves are no exception. If a religious figure appears in a tea leaf reading, this sheds light on the sitter. First, it is possible that the client is already a member of that specific religion or is considering joining or studying it. Sometimes these symbols can allude to traveling to the countries associated with these figures. I once had Jesus show up in a tea leaf reading, symbolically of course, and as the reading proceeded, the client confirmed that she was taking a trip to Jerusalem.

Also, it could be that these Ascended Masters are coming in at this time in the sitter's life to help her work through something spiritually. These figures can be called upon to bring help or insight into a situation. It might just be that the client already works with these beings, and this is simply a confirmation of that fact.

RING

Marriage (if at top of cup), long engagement (if near bottom)

Let's make a distinction between a circle (page 57) and a ring within the tea leaves. A circle is just that. A round open-holed shape of the leaves, whereas a ring has circular shape and some type of stone on top of it. The stone distinguishes it from a simple circle or a chain of circles. A ring is synonymous with marriage and commitment. The nearer to the top of the cup, the more secure the relationship. Also, if the sitter is not yet married and wondering if a proposal is in the near future, this is a definite yes.

If the ring appears farther down the cup, the commitment may not be as firm as the sitter would like. This can also indicate there may be an engagement—but a long one. If this symbol appears alongside a chain (page 53) or bells (page 41), a wedding is guaranteed. If the client is not in a relationship, then this wedding refers to someone else close to the client, and the event itself must be important in the client's life if it is showing up in the tea leaves.

TIP Remember, no symbol shows up by chance. Spirit places each one for a purpose and reason.

ROSE

Popularity, possible marriage, deepening love

There is an expression that says, "Give me my roses while I am still here." It means not to wait until people are gone before realizing how important they are in your life. Roses have long been associated with recognition. Stage actors often receive them after a performance. They are given as emblems of love between partners. Roses frequently are given when someone wins a contest or automobile races. When a rose appears in the tea leaves, it represents popularity. This is a great sign if the sitter would like to go viral online or expand her business's reach. This would also be a great symbol for a budding politician.

If the sitter enquires about the possibility of marriage or receiving a proposal, the chances are high of it coming to pass when this symbol appears. If the client is in a relationship, this is a beautiful sign that the love will deepen between the two of them. It is also a good sign that a reunion could happen between estranged lovers, especially if paired with a heart (page 78) or table (page 117).

SCALES

Legal issues, judgment, looking for balance, Libra

Lady Justice famously raises her scales high, representing a court's impartiality. Scales are forever intertwined with the legal system. The same is true when they are found in the tea leaves. The sitter may have an active court case at the time of the reading or one that will occur in the future. This can cover any matter of legal issue, from divorce to criminal proceedings. Based on accompanying symbols, in some cases, the outcome of the case can be determined, but be careful with those type of predictions, as you don't want to give the client false hope or fear.

Scales can also represent judgment and/or karma. What goes around comes around, right? See where the scales appear within the cup. If facing and near the handle, then this may be some karma the client will experience. However, if it appears farther away from the handle and toward the bottom of the cup, karma is coming for someone that has wronged the client in some way.

The scales could simply show that the sitter needs some balance in her life. Maybe the client is trying to juggle too many tasks at once. When the scales show up in this context, it is a sign for the sitter to find some stability. The zodiac sign of Libra is also represented by the scales. So, if someone else is on the sitter's mind, this could indicate who it is. It is also possible that Libra's attributes would help this situation get resolved by looking at both sides of things, looking for a fair resolution for all parties, and adding a little humor to lighten up the situation.

SCISSORS

Something cut out, fights, friend loss, sickness,
misunderstandings, confusion, possible separation

Some symbols are not individually positive, but within the full tea leaf reading, they play an important part. Such is the case with this symbol. What are scissors used for? To cut something, right? So, when a pair of scissors appears in the teacup, there may be a loss of sorts on the horizon for the sitter. First, the sitter may need to be the one to cut something from her life. There may be individuals or situations the client needs to leave behind. This symbol can show up at a transition point in the client's life. Usually, the client knows this needs to happen, but may be putting it off. As this symbol can also point to fights and the loss of friends, the changes become somewhat inevitable over time.

Scissors can also indicate a sickness that separates the sitter from good health for a while, possible fights that separate and cut out peace, even a friend loss, which, of course, removes this person from the sitter's life.

Misunderstandings and confusion come along with the scissors symbol as well. Because this symbol shows up when there is a lot of surrounding chaos, it makes sense that the sitter may be feeling unclear. Once action is taken by the sitter, the situations normally clear up soon after.

SNAKE

Enemies/caution needed, sickness, bad luck

Snakes are not the cuddliest of creatures, and they have become synonymous with someone to distrust. So, this may not be the most pleasant or positive symbol, but it does serve its purpose to warn the sitter that all things may not be as they seem. Friends may not be as they appear, and instead, they are playing a snake-in-the-grass role. Advise the sitter to utilize caution, especially in dealing with people she might already suspect.

A snake in the cup can also be an indication of sickness. Again, a reader does not need to offer medical advice, but this may simply be pointing to an existing condition the client is already aware of. Surrounding symbols will lend clarity. Snakes also represent some bad luck for the sitter. If a question comes up about starting a business or taking some type of risk, unless outnumbered by more positive symbols, I would advise the sitter to wait or at least use some caution before proceeding.

TIP If the client is not aware of any illness, simply counsel there is a potential, but *always* recommend that she seek medical treatment for all medical issues.

SNOWFLAKE

Unique, one-of-a-kind opportunity, beauty, optimism

It is said that snowflakes are as unique as fingerprints, each one unlike any other. When a snowflake appears in the teacup, the sitter is facing a unique or once-in-a-lifetime opportunity. There may be a specialized job that only the sitter is qualified for. Equally, the sitter may receive a chance to do something that only comes around once in a lifetime. When a snowflake is spotted in the tea leaves, it is a grand reassurance that this chance is one worth taking.

Alternatively, snowflakes also represent beauty, which can refer to the client herself, but usually it is in reference to the beauty of life. Depending on the surrounding symbols, the snowflake may suggest that the client is in a beautiful position in life.

Also, snowflakes mean optimism. This is a positive omen that indicates a turn in not only the sitter's current situation but also how the sitter will perceive the situation. This symbol usually shows up when the sitter has been feeling down for a while. With the appearance of this omen, that frown gets turned upside down pretty quickly.

SPIDER

Cunning, ensnarement, creating wealth

Spiders are known for patiently weaving webs to capture all sorts of things. Laying a trap to capture prey takes a fair amount of smarts. Seeing a spider in the teacup means something similar. First, this can allude to the sitter herself. This person may be intelligent and clever. However, this can also refer to another person in the sitter's life. Look for any letters (page 90) or additional symbols that would lead to that conclusion. If that is the case, there may be some deception on this person's part.

As a spider catches a fly, when found in the teacup, the spider can also refer to ensnarement. Again, if there are symbols showing deception, such as a bat (page 38) or knife (page 86) toward the client, then advise caution, as someone in the client's life may be trying to lay some type of trap. Although this sounds like spy movie antics, it basically refers to someone leading the sitter astray through lies or gossip. It is more about the sitter having an untrustworthy person around rather than a secret ploy to ruin the sitter's life.

Alternatively, a spider represents creating wealth in the client's life, since spiders weave their webs so slowly and methodically. Over time, all sorts of delightful things can be trapped in it. When this symbol comes up in the cup, it is a reminder to the sitter that she, too, can bring abundance and goodness into her life through patience and consistency.

SQUARE

Limitation, obstacle

Ever felt boxed in? Feels like being trapped, right? Squares are unforgiving shapes that limit flexibility. When a square appears in the teacup, there could be some limitations or obstacles in the sitter's way. Take a look at the overall picture the cup presents. The square may represent a past situation in which the sitter felt held back but now feels free to express herself. A square has a tendency to show up in a reading when the sitter finds herself in a rather toxic relationship. The client may feel as if she cannot fully be herself or her partner may be too controlling. This is usually a message from Spirit that they are aware of this situation and, most likely, when all the symbols are taken into account, will offer a way for the sitter to get out of it.

The sitter may also be attempting to accomplish a big goal, and there are some obstacles standing in her way. If this symbol appears with a mountain (page 96), it represents that while there will be challenges, ultimately the sitter will come out on top. As always, take in the entire scene and notice if there are more positives than negatives. If a symbol falls inside a square, which is rare, it will enhance its meaning. Apply all the LAWS (page 19).

STAR

Wish coming true, good luck, special occasion

An easy way to remember this one is to think about what wishes are made on. This is an extremely good omen. When a star appears in the tea leaves, the sitter has the chance for a wish to come true. This may be regarding a dream relationship, job, house, or whatever wish the sitter has been waiting to come true. If the remaining symbols are favorable to this one, it is an excellent reading.

If that was not enough, seeing a star in the tea leaves is also a sign of good luck. Perhaps the client has had a bout of bad luck, and this represents better days ahead or that things will go the client's way. Advise the client it is time to take a leap of faith or start something new. When Lady Luck pays a visit, seize the moment.

A star can also mean a special occasion may be on the horizon for the sitter. When coupled with a ring (page 106) and a heart (page 78), it points to an imminent wedding, or perhaps an upcoming birthday or anniversary. Either way, there is cause to celebrate. Based on the other symbols, you can determine the topic the star emphasizes.

SUN

Creativity, joy and success, happiness

The sun god, Ra, was a deity in ancient Egypt. He was called the Bringer of Light, worshipped for his warmth and life-giving properties. Since those days long ago, the sun has remained a shining example of positivity.

When the sun begins to rise, so too do the creative juices. There is something about the golden rays dancing through the day that seems to inspire anyone to create art. When the sun appears among the tea leaves, the sitter is due for a period of creativity. The sitter may soon experience a burst of creativity or creative projects may prove to be successful during this time.

The sun also appears to announce that joy and success are on the way. This could come in the form of a baby announcement, wedding proposal, or job promotion. Whatever projects the client has been working on or wants to begin will be met with success.

The client will soon experience happiness as well, most likely as a result of the forthcoming success. There is nothing better than the sun peeking through the clouds to drive away the rain, and similarly, the sun within the teacup shows the client's sad days are moving behind her. Advise the client that much brighter days are ahead and that whatever question is being inquired about will most likely have a positive outcome.

SWORD

Lovers' quarrel, threat, protection

Swords have long been associated with battles. Imagine a duel in which two rivals fight over a lover. Picture a swashbuckling buccaneer making a daring escape from a gang of pirates armed only with his sword. Although swords are not used as weapons as much these days, every branch of the military still employs them ceremonially. When seen in a teacup, the sword represents a quarrel between two lovers. This is not a pleasant symbol to get in terms of one's current relationship. It is most likely filled with bickering and disagreements when a sword appears.

This is another symbol where the LAWS (page 19) play an important part in deciphering the full meaning. If the sword is pointing toward the handle, there could be a threat aimed at the sitter, but this does not necessarily mean there is a risk of physical danger to the sitter. This can simply represent someone gossiping about the client or a workplace situation that has turned sour. Counsel the client to be cautious, especially of anyone she may already be having issues with. However, if the sword is pointing away from the handle, the client will be protected from any would-be harm.

TABLE

Social gatherings, reunion, party

The best memories in life usually involve sitting around a table. Whether big ones or small ones, eating and laughing with friends, lovers, family, schoolmates, and work colleagues are good times. Tables are also excellent meeting places. So, it is no surprise that a table in a teacup indicates upcoming social gatherings for the sitter. For example, there could be a work function the sitter will attend that is advantageous to her career. Maybe a friend is holding a get-together, and it is there that the sitter meets the love of her life. When this symbol appears, I urge the sitter to go out, even if she is introverted and usually hates gatherings. The table shows up to make one aware that this is not just any old hangout. This meeting has the potential to change the course of someone's life.

A table in the tea leaves also signifies a reunion. The sitter may be attending her high school or college reunion in the near future. It can also indicate a reunion between the sitter and an ex-flame or old friend, which can occur due to chance or by a planned meeting. A table also means a party. Perhaps there is a birthday or anniversary to celebrate. Look to surrounding symbols to fill in any blanks.

TREE

Recovery of health, prosperity, wish granted

Trees are the great givers of life. They exhale precious oxygen that helps clear the air, and they supply the world with fruit and vegetation. For this reason, seeing a tree in the teacup is a symbol of the sitter's health returning to normal. As always, do not make a diagnosis, but do relay the message that her health should be improving. Any advice more than that should be addressed by a medical professional only.

A tree also represents incoming prosperity for the client. Based on the shape and size of the tree, the amount of wealth the client can expect can be ascertained. If it is closer to the cup's rim, the increased abundance will happen soon. If it is farther into the cup, the wait may be a while longer.

If the sitter is feeling especially hopeful and dreaming big, this is the time to take action because trees are a sign of wishes granted. Trees are great signs that whatever the sitter has been manifesting (page 25) will soon to come to pass. When this symbol appears, the sitter may want to start manifesting (if she has not already) because as a tree grows and branches out, so too do manifestations when the timing is divine.

TRIANGLE

Good fortune from an unexpected source, good sign

A grand pyramid graces the back of every US one-dollar bill and represents strength and prosperity, which makes it an ideal emblem for money. Seeing a triangle in the tea leaves portends good fortune from, most likely, an unexpected source. This could be lottery winnings, a lucky streak in Vegas or Atlantic City, a long-lost uncle's inheritance, or even an unexpected tax refund. I have begun seeing this symbol for social media influencers who have caught the eye of brands and get offered a deal shortly thereafter. The key to remember is that this good fortune will come from some unpredicted source.

The triangle is always a good sign. Look to see if the triangle contains other symbols within it. If so, those symbols' meanings will be magnified and strengthened per the LAWS (page 19). For example, if an anchor (page 33) appears within a triangle, the sitter will not only be sure to achieve business success but also do so in a way that is beyond even her wildest dreams. The triangle increases the power of any symbol it surrounds and adds to its positivity.

UMBRELLA

In need of shelter

When an umbrella appears in the cup, more than tea may be brewing. Most likely, there is possible trouble in the sitter's life. An umbrella shields from the pouring rain and beating sun. It acts as a form of protection. In a tea leaf reading, the umbrella appears to alert the sitter that protection is needed. However, the manner in which it appears will determine if the sitter will receive it or not.

Let's pull out those trusty LAWS (page 19). Start with the appearance. If the umbrella is open, protection is on the way. For example, this may be an unexpected check that covers mounting bills. It could be a lease approval right in the nick of time. However, if the umbrella is closed, protection may not show up in time. Precautions need to be taken now. This is one of those sensitive symbols that could indicate the sitter is in physical danger, such as in the case of domestic violence. Remember, not all symbols are positive, but their intentions are: Their aim is to inform and educate the client. Again, this is not to be read as a singular meaning. With surrounding symbols, the overall message may be much more hopeful.

TIP A tea leaf reading should serve as a safe space for the sitter. She should feel comfortable in sharing sensitive information and have the confidence that anything discussed within the reading will remain confidential. Although a tea leaf reader is not a licensed professional, readings should always be conducted in a qualified manner.

UNICORN

Take your dreams seriously

A unique and mystical creature, the unicorn evokes all sorts of images for people, such as one-of-kind dreams, and everyone carries some with them. When the unicorn shows up in a tea leaf reading, the message is loud and clear. It is time to take those dreams seriously! When I see this symbol in a reading, I know that my sitter is in need of a pep talk. This person has major goals, but something is holding her back. Depending on the neighboring symbols, I can usually work out what it is. Sometimes the sitter will share this information during the course of the reading.

The unicorn is a special emblem that Spirit chooses to use to not only encourage the client to go after her dreams but also point out that, although what someone may want to do sounds exactly like what someone else is already doing, there is room for everyone. It is similar to tea leaf reading. What I may see and how I interpret those images can be completely different from how you might perceive them. And that is okay. In fact, it is encouraged. So, although the dream may be similar to someone else's, the execution of it will be different based on the person attempting it. Encourage the client that this is the moment to step up and chase those big moments in life. No more sitting on the sidelines. The power of the unicorn will guide the sitter to achieve those dreams.

WAGON

Something approaches, inheritance, wedding

Wagons are as connected to the Romany as horses (page 79) are. Both are used to transport us from place to place. Think of the wagons used to journey through the American West. Just as the Romany did, the pioneers carried their entire lives within those wagons. When found in the teacup, a wagon indicates something is approaching and refers to a change coming to the sitter's life. It can mean that a physical visitation will take place, but often it refers to a shift in the sitter's life, such as a change of job or residence. Overall, a wagon refers to an energetic swing coming for the client.

It can also represent that the client is receiving an inheritance. Kings used to carry their treasures with them in wagons. Depending on the other symbols in the cup, this may be the case for the client. It also possible that the wagon means a wedding is soon to take place. If the wagon is accompanied by a ring (page 106) or bells (page 41), this is practically guaranteed.

WAGON WHEEL

Movement, progress is coming, turning point, unexpected gift

The Romany love a wagon wheel. In fact, it is so important to us that it appears on our flag, nestled right in the center of it, as a red sixteen-spoked chakra between the green for earth and the blue for heaven. It not only represents the Romany's Indian origins but also expresses movement and the burst of fire from which all creation began.

When a wheel appears in the tea leaves, there will be movement in the sitter's life. There may be a physical change of residence. This can also mean, however, that the sitter's life will start to feel like it is moving forward again. It normally shows up when things have gone stale. It is a chance for fresh energy.

So, progress will take place, although it may not come as swiftly as the client would like. Check the location of the wagon wheel within the cup. If the wagon wheel is near the rim, this forward momentum will start soon, no later than a couple of weeks. Found within the middle of the cup, the progress may not pick up for a few months, and if the wagon wheel appears at the bottom of the cup, things might stay a little slow until the next year. A little patience may need to be exercised while the wheels begin to turn. More than likely, this will become a turning point in the sitter's life. This symbol shows up for the big moments. Check surrounding symbols to get more clarity on exactly what. This also could be an unexpected gift that gets things moving for the sitter.

WAND

Magic is possible, manifestation

All great wizards and witches have carried wands. They are the devices through which all of their magic could be channeled and made manifest. The same can be said when finding a wand in the teacup, as it represents that magic is possible at that moment in time. This is a message from Spirit that the sitter would be wise to heed. If the client is hesitant about the meaning, she simply needs to be reminded of her innate magic. Each person carries the ability to create the life of their dreams. Sometimes, though, life can help you forget that, as it can become a heavy experience day to day. This normally shows up to reinspire the sitter and ignite a fire within her to get started on her dreams.

Additionally, this is an excellent sign for manifesting (page 25). When the wand shows up in the tea leaves, the client has the energy of the Universe flowing behind her in order to make those dreams a reality. It does not matter if the client has ever tried manifesting before or not. This works for first-timers as well as seasoned pros.

WITCH

Inner strength, wisdom, magic

Witches have gotten a bad rap for thousands of years. Charged with claims of bewitching cattle, seducing spouses, and dancing with the devil, historical witches have always been labeled as "nasty women." However, what many (i.e., the patriarchy) failed to see is that these were simply women who knew in their bones how crops grew, which herbs to use, and that it was best not to start new projects during a full moon (that is what new moons are for). So, seeing a witch in the tea leaves is nothing to fear. Instead, it is definitely a positive sign that refers to the sitter's inner strength. This is probably a moment in the client's life in which she will need to lean on her inner strength to make it through a tough time—but use the surrounding symbols to gain clarity.

A witch in the teacup also represents wisdom. Again, much like strength, this refers to the client's wisdom. The client most likely is a friend who always gives great advice. This person is someone other people count on for guidance. Also, a witch omen indicates magic. Maybe it appears in the cup as a reminder to the sitter to use her magic again. The witch tends to show up when a sitter feels repressed, when a part of her identity is not being fully expressed in some way. Being authentic is true magic, as there is not another human being like you on this planet.

WOLF

Guard against jealous friends, clever, strength

Wolves are highly intelligent animals that run in packs. They have realized through years of evolution that is easier to get tasks accomplished when each wolf helps the group. In the rare instance that one of the wolves is not a good hunter and cannot provide for the overall group, the pack kicks this wolf out. It is not personal; rather, it is simply needed for survival. So, when the wolf shows up in a tea leaf reading, it is a warning to the sitter that a friend has become jealous. When this happens, the overall health of a relationship decreases, much like when one wolf does not pull its weight for the pack. The sitter may be at a crossroads and now is the time to re-evaluate whether this friendship is healthy or not.

Additionally, a wolf indicates that the sitter is clever. The news about a potentially jealous friend may not catch this client off guard. This person is no one's fool. This omen relates to the sitter's strength. This trait will come in handy when the sitter has to deal with the jealous individuals in her life. This is especially true if the wolf is also accompanied by a pig (page 102). The sitter may recently have had a run of good luck that caused some already not-so-true friends to become envious.

WOMAN

Visitor with good news, happiness

The symbol of a woman is a little more complex than its male counterpart. Seeing a woman in the tea leaves means a visitor is coming with good news. Most often, the information the sitter receives is for her. For example, a colleague stops by to inform the client of a promotion. The sitter can also simply receive a visitor who has exciting news to share, such as an upcoming wedding or pregnancy. As with the symbol of a man (page 93) in the tea leaves, the gender of the symbol does not mean that the actual visitor will also be that same gender. It simply means a person will pay the sitter a visit. Also, the tea leaves evolve to reflect the world around it. A visit does not necessarily have to occur in person, but can be virtual through an online meeting.

Alternatively, when a woman appears in the teacup, the client is destined for happiness. The surrounding symbols will point to which area of life this is in reference to, but I find that it tends to relate to joy within relationships, with a significant other, and also to self.

ZODIAC SIGNS

Aries, Taurus, Gemini, Cancer, Leo, Virgo, Libra, Scorpio,
Sagittarius, Capricorn, Aquarius, Pisces

When seeing the signs of the zodiac, many definitions can be given. **One:** The sitter or someone the sitter is inquiring about was born under that sign of the zodiac. **Two:** The sitter or someone the sitter is asking about has the attributes of this zodiac sign. **Three:** The energy of this zodiac sign may be describing the current situation in the client's life. For example, if the sign for Taurus appears in the cup, is the situation or environment the sitter's dealing with obstinate, stubborn, and seemingly immovable? Then bingo, you have your explanation for that omen appearing in the teacup. Following is a brief summary of the twelve zodiac signs, their characteristics. and how they may relate to a tea leaf reading.

Aries (fire sign). Attributes include short temper, impulsive, natural leader, and courageous. As the fiery first sign of the zodiac, an Aries in the teacup can mean things are moving in the sitter's life. The situation at hand may need action and go, go, go without much worry for future consequences. These meanings also apply when you see a ram.

Taurus (earth sign). Attributes include stubborn, hardworking, loyal, and independent. The ever-steady Taurus can indicate that the situation at hand feels immovable, but with hard work and persistence, any obstacle can be overcome. These meanings also apply when you see a bull.

Gemini (air sign). Attributes include curious, gossipy, flexible, and extroverted. The light-hearted and quick-witted Gemini can refer to a situation that will require some cunning thinking to get out of. These meanings also apply when you see twins.

Cancer (water sign). Attributes include moody, nurturing, family-oriented, and trustworthy. The mother energy of the zodiac, Cancer can speak to a situation that is emotionally in flux and requires a little extra TLC to resolve. These meanings also apply when you see a crab.

Leo (fire sign). Attributes include prideful, generous, passionate, and regal. Seeing a royal Leo can indicate a situation that requires some generosity of spirit and one that may be a time of recognition for the sitter. Also see lion (page 92).

Virgo (earth sign). Attributes include critical, detail-oriented, perfectionist, and organized. The Mary Poppins of the zodiac, Virgo can suggest a situation that requires some organization, dedication, and an eye for detail to be properly sorted out. These meanings also apply when you see a maiden.

Libra (air sign). Attributes include charming, indecisive, fair, and flirtatious. When a friendly Libra appears in the teacup, a little finessing and charisma may be needed in order to smooth over the situation at hand. Also see scales (page 108).

Scorpio (water sign). Attributes include broody, secretive, insightful, and bold. Spotting a mysterious and dark Scorpio suggests a situation in which stealth and secrecy may be the best way to deal with a sticky issue. These meanings also apply when you see a scorpion.

Sagittarius (fire sign). Attributes include forceful, risk taker, straightforward, and honest. A situation may be in dire need of straight talk and no backing down if a bold Sagittarius symbol appears in a reading. These meanings also apply when you see a centaur.

Capricorn (earth sign). Attributes include ambitious, determined, structured, and workaholic. When a tenacious Capricorn appears in a reading, the situation may call for a little extra elbow grease and determination to ensure the outcome is successful. Also see goat (page 73).

Aquarius (air sign). Attributes include intelligent, unique, otherworldly, and humanitarian. Finding an elusive Aquarius within the tea leaves indicates that a situation may need some out-of-the-box thinking in order to come to a resolution that everyone can benefit from. These meanings also apply when you see a water bearer.

Pisces (water sign). Attributes include sensitive, dreamy, artistic, and escapist. The last but certainly not least sign of the zodiac, Pisces indicates a sitter may be dealing with a situation that is not all that it appears to be. Some illusions may be obscuring the truth, but taking a gentle approach can help distinguish what is false from what is true. Also see fish (page 70).

CHAPTER 5

EXAMPLE
TEA LEAF READINGS

THE FOLLOWING THREE sample readings are included to help familiarize you with real-life scenarios and their corresponding interpretations. The first two will give you a hypothetical situation that a sitter may present you with, along with the full explanation of the tea leaves. In the third example, you get to try out the role of reader firsthand. Using the glossary and your natural intuition, it's up to you to help the third sitter through her issue.

EXAMPLE 1

A client, Stephanie, arrives and sits down, looking somewhat worried. Upon sipping her tea, she states that she has one thought on her mind, *Will she marry her partner, Brian? Is he going to pop the question? Is he The One?* After swirling the cup and allowing the remaining liquid to drain, this is what the tea leaves reveal.

Will Stephanie and Brian make it official? Let's find out. We'll apply all the LAWS (page 19) to get the full picture. Let's look at the illustration of Stephanie's tea leaves in her teacup on the next page.

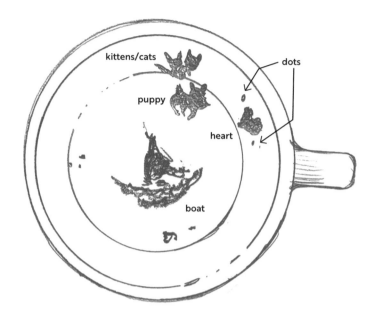

Starting at the handle, straight away there is a heart sitting beneath it. This is an amazing sign, especially in a love reading. Hearts (page 78) are an omen of love and marriage. Right out of the gate, this reading is looking pretty good. It is not the largest symbol in the cup, but it is proportional to most of the other symbols. I also see two distinct dots (page 64) sitting around the heart. Here, the dots are increasing the strength of the heart's meaning. I also like that there are only two dots, as they each seem to represent the two parties in question. I believe these two people carry unique energies and combine well as a loving couple.

Turning the cup in a clockwise direction, my eye next catches two kittens nestled closely together, one slightly larger than the other. Cats (page 52) are often seen as symbols for independence and good luck. If there were only one cat here, I would immediately begin to have doubts that Brian was the one for my client.

However, because there are two, and they are sitting so closely together, I interpret this as a great match between two people who enjoy their freedom and independence. With one kitten bigger than the other, I would infer that either one of them acts more mature than the other or that one of them takes on more of a caretaker role within the relationship. Again, taken together with the heart, these are positive symbols for a happy relationship.

Quite near the kittens, a little farther down in the cup, there is a puppy (page 62) sitting at the kittens' feet. This tells me that there is a lot of loyalty within this relationship, and I would not be surprised if their relationship did not start out as a good friendship. With that type of foundation, there's a good chance these two are going to be jumping the broom soon.

This takes us to our last symbol. At the very bottom of the cup clearly sits a pirate ship. It also happens to be the largest symbol in this reading. Boats (page 44) are excellent signs of journeys. This indicates to me that this couple will be setting sail on a life together. What greater journey is there than that of a life lived with your soulmate? This may also hint to a destination wedding. Since it is at the very bottom of the cup, I would not expect the journey to happen any sooner than a year or so out. So, after considering the entire cup, I would feel confident in telling my client that yes, indeed, I do believe Brian is the one for her and that I may not know exactly when he will propose (and who wants to spoil the surprise), but possibly within the next year, she will be off on a grand adventure as a newlywed.

EXAMPLE 2

The next client, Amber, comes in and sits down, never breaking eye contact. She makes all the usual niceties but reveals nothing. When asked if she would like to focus on a particular area of life for the tea leaf reading, she says, "Just tell me what comes up." Sounds simple, right? This is what is called a general reading. When you have an idea of what the sitter is looking for, the pictures come together more easily and make more of a story—at least initially when you are still learning. However, when someone is not interested in looking at one topic or subject and is open to whatever shows up, it can be a bit overwhelming at first. You may feel like you have to fill in more of the blanks.

Do not fear. This type of reading can be rather freeing as well. It is all about perspective. This reading allows for your intuition to kick in more because you are just interpreting the symbols as they stand without, even if subconsciously, trying to make them fit into an answer for the sitter. Following lies an illustration of a teacup of symbols from the sitter who just wants a general reading.

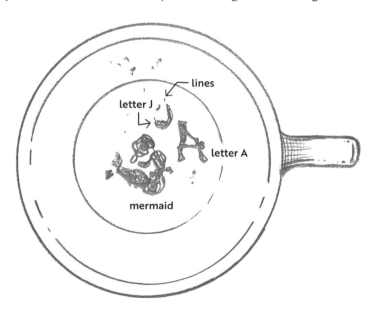

Unlike the first example, this cup seems to be sparse on symbols. That is normal. In fact, readings can vary greatly from sitter to sitter. For this reading, the first thing that stands out to me is the letter A. It also happens to be the sitter's first initial. Letters (page 90) act as initials for names and places. There is also a smaller J next to it. This could be someone the sitter is romantically attracted to or vice versa, but let's keep looking. The connection could be purely platonic. Since the J is not as large as the A, this person will aid the sitter, Amber, as she may be the one taking more of a leadership role in this enterprise.

Right above the J are two small lines (page 91). This can indicate a journey, progress, or movement. Seeing as it rests above the symbol, J most likely will be taking a short trip, possibly to travel to the sitter, or is moving closer to coming to a decision about what A is offering.

Rather close to both letters, I see a mermaid. Mermaids (page 94) in a teacup are rather special. They signify a creative phase in the sitter's life, two worlds combining, or even a trip. Sometimes these symbols can mean more than one thing at the same time. In this case, with the location so close to both the other symbols, this creative phase and possible melding of worlds seems to affect both people, Amber, and the elusive J.

All of these symbols are found at the bottom of the cup. So, this all will probably kick off within the next year or so, nothing in the immediate future. This endeavor will probably take time to build before launching. With the addition of the mermaid, I do not feel drawn to speculate that these two individuals are romantically linked, but more likely two people coming together to form something new. That takes care of two worlds melding, as well as creativity.

As you can see, you do not need a cup of a zillion symbols to have a deep reading. I would offer this meaning: There is a creative pursuit that Amber has been thinking of launching. This would bring her great satisfaction. With the initial J, it is possible she has someone in mind she would like to work with on this project. This could be a business partner or investor. This person would be receptive and would be willing to physically move closer to help or simply come together with her to accomplish this feat.

At this point, the sitter advises that in fact she has been toying with the idea of starting up a decorating business with her best friend, Jenny, but she has been hesitant. She was hopeful that the reading would serve as a sign to confirm what she needs to do. On hearing that the tea leaves foretell a creative pursuit working out well between Jenny and her, Amber is overjoyed. The client finally cracks a smile and is satisfied with her reading. Although there were not many symbols within the teacup, Spirit brought forth the exact message that the sitter needed at that particular moment in time. Remember, as the reader, it is simply your job to interpret the symbols and convey the message. From that point, it is the sitter's job to decide what, if anything, to do with that information.

EXAMPLE 3

Now it is your turn. Here is an illustration of a cup chock-full of symbols for you to interpret for your would-be sitter. Your client, Barbara, is open to whatever comes up, much like Amber in example 2. This will let you focus on the symbols as they appear and help you avoid making them fit a certain scenario. So, ready to practice for real? Here's the cup. **Hint:** Some of the tea leaf symbols are not listed in the glossary. Time to practice using your intuition and figure out what the symbols mean for you. After you interpret the illustration, flip to page 146 for my interpretation to compare notes, but no peeking ahead of time. Give it your best try!

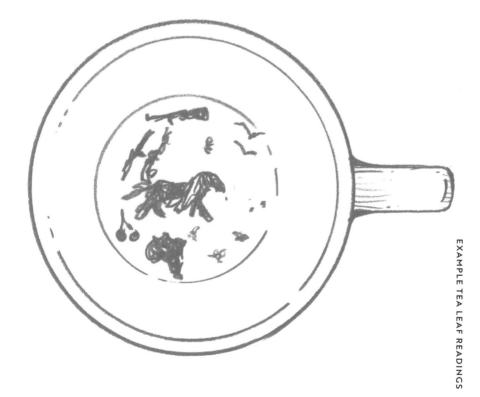

CHAPTER 6

TAKING TEA LEAF READING FURTHER

TASSEOMANCY DOES NOT have to be performed in its traditional format to help strengthen your intuition. In fact, you can use these tips to flex your psychic muscles without ever reading for a sitter.

HARNESSING YOUR INTUITION

One way is to start or end your day with a tea leaf reading, isolating a single symbol. Pick out one symbol and immediately write down what comes to you. Do not stop to think about it, just write. Get out as much as you can about that one symbol and all that it evokes for you. After you are done, check against the glossary and see if you get any matches. You may be surprised by how much clicks for you. This journal of daily readings can also become your personal glossary for future reference.

As another way to practice, pour yourself a cup each day. Do it first thing before your day has begun. Ask your cup to reveal to you how the day will unfold. Drink your tea, make notes of what you saw, and then at the end of the day, pull out a journal and compare notes. Did everything you see turn out to be true for that day? Can you see where you may have misinterpreted some symbols and know for the next time how to self-correct? Everything is energy and time occurring all at once. So, use this practice to feel into the energies of the world. You can even go beyond your personal day's events and ask the cup to show you what may be going on in your town, nation, or even the world that day. Each cup is like a newspaper fresh off the press, and you are the one who gets to read the first edition.

You can also practice with friends and family to look into their current life situations. The trick with intuition is learning to trust yourself. No matter how kooky or off topic what you see or what impression you receive is, say it. It starts to train your brain to allow your intuition to shine through. Each time you do, it gets stronger and stronger. It does not matter if you think you sound or look ridiculous. This will also help you in your daily life. The stronger your intuition and the more you trust your gut instincts, the less likely you are to move away from your true path in life. You will make decisions and stick with them.

ADDITIONAL USES

Tea leaf reading obviously taps into psychic awareness and abilities, but it can also be used for mediumship development. Mediumship is the practice of connecting with those who have passed away. As with most intuitive practices, it is all about intentions. Before you brew a cup, set the intention that you will focus on connecting with loved ones in spirit during the reading. This activity may be easier at first with a friend or family member, as reading for oneself is often difficult for even the most advanced practitioner because objectivity is hard to come by. There is a lot to play on your self-doubts. However, with a friend or partner, set the intention of connecting with their loved ones on the other side and see what comes up. Numbers and letters represent the spirit's name and birthdate or date of passing. The symbols that come up can be evidence of the person's life or how they passed, each being a clue that helps bring this person back to life, so to speak, as more and more of their personality is revealed in the reading. Many mediums working today did not start out working directly as mediums. Instead, they started as a tarot card reader, an oracle reader, or yes, even a tea leaf reader.

HOW TO HANDLE A "BAD" READING

Nothing in life is all gum drops and lollipops. There are going to be readings that do not give sitters a happily ever after, such as lotto numbers or their one true love coming along. So, how does one go about breaking the bad news from the cup? It is all in perspective. Most times, we all receive clues from the Universe before things go bad. We receive little nudges along the way that a situation may not end well if we keep heading in a particular direction. For example, your partner's jealousy issues may make you uncomfortable, but you dismiss those feelings and decide it's just their way of showing they love you. Or you may get a sinking feeling in your gut every time you head to the office, but you chalk it up to your morning coffee and head in anyway. So, when the cup lays out things for the sitter in a cut-and-dry manner, it can be hard to know how to frame it. To begin with, as Shakespeare wrote in *Hamlet*, "There is nothing either good or bad, but thinking makes it so." Although you may have to tell the sitter that they are not in fact going to get that new job they applied for, it does not mean there isn't something better waiting. For example, if I did not see a new relationship on the horizon for a client, I would simply explain that while no one is coming in at this time, it does not mean there is no room for love.

Usually, the Universe keeps us out of relationships for our own good. It is a marker that we need to work on loving ourselves first. This would be where the maxim applies: As soon as you stop looking, love finds you. In truth, what happens is that you are busy loving yourself and teaching the Universe what type of love you deserve, and then the Universe has its marching orders to bring it to you. This definitely changes the tone of the reading. It is a lot better to explain this for the sitter than to say, "Sorry, no partner for you right now."

Another example is that of a sitter who comes to you wanting to know if she is going to get the job that she applied for a few weeks back. This happens often. If the tea leaves do not look promising, search the other symbols for advice to offer. More times than not, another bigger, better offer will come for the sitter.

THROWING A TEA LEAF READING PARTY

Here is an idea for when you are feeling adventurous. Get a group of like-minded people together and host a tea leaf reading party! You can go all out. Get snacks, finger sandwiches, beautiful teacup sets, and chocolates. Gather for a holiday or special occasion. This makes a great bachelorette party starter. You have all the participants together. Everyone can take a sneak peek into their lives and then they can head off to the after-party. It also makes a great birthday party or get-together. I've also found it works for couples. If nothing else, it makes a great date-night activity, especially if the leaves portend romance. If they are not that good, simply give a disclaimer upfront that you are not responsible for what the tea leaves bring.

Let your mind go wild. Decorate the room however you wish. This works great at Halloween. Do make sure you are culturally sensitive. "Gypsy" costumes are definitely a no-no. As you now know, the Romany people helped spread and increase the popularity of this divinatory practice, and it is more than okay to do tea leaf readings. It is not a closed practice. However, as always, be respectful of any culture that is not yours. Continuing the tradition in a respectful manner is one of the greatest ways to honor the Romany people. My ancestors have assured me that they definitely approve.

ANSWER TO EXAMPLE 3

This is my tea leaf reading interpretation for example 3 on page 139. There is a lot happening in Barbara's life. I would first address the not-so-great parts. There is a gun (page 74) pointing away from the handle located near the top of the cup. This indicates there is some type of strife happening presently. Seeing the letter H (page 90), my bet would be that it has something to do with someone with the first initial H. Because the gun is pointing away from the handle, Barbara's hands are not necessarily clean in this friction.

One of the largest symbols in this cup is a horse (page 79). Horses refer to good news and a journey, as well as close friendships. Due to the horse's proximity to the H, I believe this alludes to H and Barbara's relationship as good friends who seem to be going through a rough patch. Barbara most likely has her guard up, and there is an issue of trust involved.

The next symbol that jumped out at me were a couple of cherries to the left of the H. Cherries are not included in this glossary, but what does this fruit evoke for you? I find them to be beautiful and shiny on the outside, but if you have never had cherries, you would have no clue as to the hard pits hidden inside. Could these represent a peace offering of sorts between H and Barbara that is not as genuine as it may first seem? What is your instinct?

The remaining symbols I found were two birds (page 43) and the continent of Africa. These, along with the horse, all point to travel, and in this case, the trip is most likely to Africa or at the very least a different country. The journey will probably offer Barbara a chance to clear her head regarding her current friendship issues and return ready to move forward. She may also receive good news while she is away, as both the bird and horse represent that.

Again, you may have found all of these, perhaps only a few, none at all, or maybe saw something else entirely. Remember the mantra, *What I see is meant for me.* The point is that what my eye caught led me to deliver the message Spirit intended. Did you come to similar conclusions? If you did not this time, it is okay. I have a feeling you did get at least some of it, and that is a great place to build from.

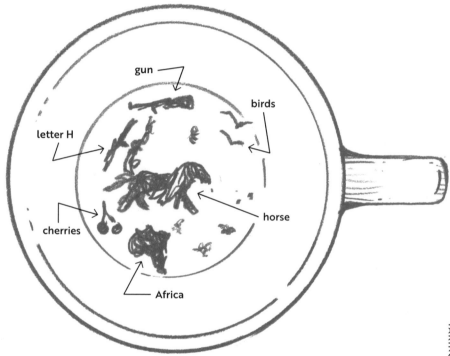

CONCLUSION

You now have all the tools and resources you need to become a pro at discerning the symbols within the tea leaves. You can brew a cup whenever you need a little guidance or direction for your day—or take it a step further and invite the whole gang over for a tea leaf reading party! Let this become a meditative practice. Zone in to your inner guidance system, and allow it to help you decipher the messages within the leaves for you and others. Remain a casual dabbler of divination or hone your skills to become a paid professional. All the pieces are there. My part of this story is now over. I happily leave you to begin telling yours, not only for yourself but also for those who trust you with theirs.

ACKNOWLEDGMENTS

This project would not have been possible without my dear editor, John Foster, reaching out and getting this grand adventure started. I am forever in his debt for making a dream of mine come true. I would also like to acknowledge the tremendous love and support my husband and children have given me. They are my biggest cheerleaders and greatest inspirations. Last, but certainly not least, I have to express my gratitude to Spirit, who I know conspired from beyond the veil to bring all of this to fruition. Thank you from the bottom of my heart. I hope this work makes you proud.

ABOUT THE AUTHOR

 April Wall is an international psychic medium with twenty years of experience helping clients sort through life's ups and downs. A proud Romany, she carries on the traditions started by the strong women in her family, especially her great-grandmother, great-aunt, and granny, or as she refers to them, April's Angels. She lives with her husband, two kids, two doggies, and one spoiled kitty. Find her online at namastemagical.com to book a reading, and keep up to date through her social media accounts by following her on Instagram and TikTok @namastemagical.

INDEX